An Alternative Perspective on Education

An Alternative Perspective on Education

Atul Kothari

PRABHAT PRAKASHAN

Published by
PRABHAT PRAKASHAN PVT. LTD.
4/19 Asaf Ali Road,
New Delhi-110 002 (INDIA)
e-mail: prabhatbooks@gmail.com

ISBN 978-93-90923-97-7
AN ALTERNATIVE PERSPECTIVE ON EDUCATION
by Shri Atul Kothari

Edition
2024

Price
₹ 500.00 (Rupees Five Hundred only)

Printed at
R-Tech Offset Printers, Delhi

Explore Solution, Not Problem

हिमगिरि के उत्तुंग शिखर पर,
बैठ शिला की शीतल छाँह;
एक पुरुष भीगे नयनों से,
देख रहा था प्रलय प्रवाह!

(कामायनी, जयशंकर प्रसाद, चिंतासर्ग)

Atop towering summit of Himgiri,
Sitting in cool shadow of rock;
A man with moist eyes,
Watched the surge of doom!
(*Kamayani, Jayashankar Prasad, Chinta Sarg*)

Despite being dependent on the principles and concepts of philosophy, psychology etc., eduction is inherently, and naturally, a societal process. This is the reason, every nation is, or wishes to be, conscious and alert about stability and development of its society. But the truth greater than this is that every society, not only at its different levels, but also in its varying complexions, is in itself a virtual synonym of intricate composition. Consequently, every nation, society, family, school etc, have in their compositional texture, perpetually complex mutual relation. It is obvious that in the process of evolving policies, such a complex inter-relation cannot be ignored. This too is apparent that in order to understand their intricate mutual relation, that social attitude needs to be understood which develops such intricacy. Along with this, it is imperative to sense the aroma of the soil of that society from which such compositions grow and develop. Study of decisions regarding education, and their modes, cannot be isolated from this societal process. In order to understand this societal process, it becomes nearly essential to know as to which social forces, for which reasons, and in which ways, influence education. In other words, we need to identify those elements and the regulatory role they play in determining the distinct character and nature of education. Apart from this, it also becomes nearly essential to ponder over the facts as to how social complexities that come up, or changed social situations, influence the distinct character and nature of education.

In volatile social situation, a peculiar experience is coming up regarding education—education, usually viewed as a means of solving social problems, and traditionally considered facilitator of multi-dimensional evolution of human life or a powerful instrument effecting realisation of creative capabilities inherent in man in natural way, is, in present times, itself helplessly looking for mature efforts to put it on the right track of development. And this too is a fact that education is itself desperately crying for a saviour. The group of people struggling with these situations in the ever changeable society, spontaneously turns towards education to resolve myriads of contemporary issues troubling it. Men begin to see the whole canvas of education as an effective and permanent troubleshooter for multi-dimensional issues facing the society. This tendency eventually converts into a wistful longing. Educationists related to the field of education begin to view the 'issues and assumptions', which are forcefully deemed to be 'conclusions of research', as 'educational principles with sluggish movement'. But they fail to induce momentum to education. As a result of this, people, upset with slow movement of education begin to consider it responsible for all problems. As a result of this, people get upset with education, which always struggles with social conflicts and contradictions as its intrinsic nature, and blame education itself for all problems. This creates an aura of mistrust about the educational process, necessitating dialogue and discourse in order to clear the cloud.

In the prevailing situation, education, with a view to adding momentum to its growth, wistfully waits for jealous and struggle-oriented thinkers who trust education, and who can stride in co-ordination with it, and, in due course, heal the deep distress it is plagued with. Education also keeps waiting for selfless strugglers who can light up its path ahead.

The present book, while discussing, and communicating in simple language, how to struggle with struggles for lighting up the path of education, puts forth solutions instead of listing problems and, thereby, convinces us of its efficacy as a creative effort to ameliorate education.

It is true that education is a dynamic process which feeds on experience. Live experience is the best way of understanding this process, and also giving it a right direction. Judged from this view, this book deserves special status. Shri Atul Kothari is the author of this book. He has thoroughly understood the nature as well as properties of society and education through his direct experience and encounters with relevant issues. On the basis of such a rich understanding of education, he has been making through his speeches and articles, zealous and honest efforts to explore the right direction of education. The main feature of his style is to carve and pinpoint in plain language, the complex nature of education, and to generate balance among educational activities, so that education, while giving to society a co-ordinated texture, may infuse ingenuity in its cultural and creative strength. This implies the fulfilment of an onerous responsibility towards society.

Atulji believes that 'if country is to be changed, education has to be changed'. This is the thesis enumerated in this book. All the articles included in this book elaborate various dimensions of this very thesis. The first chapter of the book—Educational Change in Bharat: Needs and Direction—

very precisely highlights its objectives. In this chapter, the writer, while logically examining the nature of education and explaining the justification of educational change, successfully elucidates as to why after all, such a change is required and in which shape and form? This chapter, in fact, puts forth the gist of objectives mentioned in the essays of the whole book. This too is a matter of intensive research that 'mother-tongue' is the centripetal issue for educational change.

Environment and character building, intended for physical and mental cleanliness of society, may be seen as the defining background of the book. The special elaboration of the cultural value of Kumbh, and brief biography of Srinivasa Ramanujan, distinguished mathematician, are both inspiring and touching. However, the remarkable proposals regarding various aspects of education are expected to be implemented.

In a nutshell, the entire material of the book reveals the author's concern as well as thinking regarding education, reinforcing credence to the dictum—'find out solution, not problems'. I have every hope that the author's present work will accomplish its responsibility in the world of education and will keep inspiring him to continuously move ahead as the Vedas exhorted चरैवेति, चरैवेति (move on, keep moving on). With these hopes and wishes

चलता था धीरे-धीरे
वह एक यात्रियों का दल,
सरिता के रम्य पुलिन में,
गिरि-पथ से ले निज संबल॥

(कामायनी, आनंदसर्ग)

Walked leisurely with provisions
That one bunch of pilgrims,
By charming bank of stream
Amidst mountain valley

(Kamayani, Anandsarg)

—Chandkiran

Preface

On August 15, 1947 the tricolour was hoisted in place of the Union Jack, but the necessary changes were not made in the management of the country. The central subject implied here is the educational management. Post-Independence, it was expected that the nature and texture of the country's education would be in harmony with social and national necessities in Bharatiya perspective. But it never happened. We believe that the root of the majority of problems of the country lies in faulty education system. As such, radical change in the education system of the country should be the subject of prime importance.

In course of the Independence Movement, our great leaders-including Mahamana Madan Mohan Malaviya, Maharshi Aurobindo, Gurudev Rabindranath Thakur, Mahatma Gandhi, Acharya Vinoba Bhave, etc., effectively struggled, for replacing the prevailing education system with pragmatic alternatives. In the same way, spiritual stalwarts like Swami Vivekananda, Swami Dayananda Saraswati, Bhagini Nivedita, etc., also contemplated on the issue of transforming education system. They also attempted at creating some functional models to exemplify their ideas regarding education.

After Independence, unfortunately, the opinions of all these iconic thinkers were set aside, and the education system set up by the British, with minor modifications from time to time, was retained in perpetuity. This may be for two important reasons:

- The system set up by the British was suitable for the ruling elite and the so-called upper classes. Hence, continuance of this system was convenient for them.
- After Independence, the control and leadership of educational administration rested in the hands of non-Bharatiya aliens.

As a result, whatever modifications were attempted in education, they in most of the cases, lacked direction. Their vision was non-Bharatiya and, therefore, not appropriate for the country's needs.

Post-Independence, for the first time Radhakrishnan Commission was constituted in 1949 for higher education. In 1952, Mudaliar Commission was constituted for secondary education. In 1964, Kothari Commission was constituted for Samagra Shiksha, i.e, education at all levels. But no commission was constituted with special focus on primary education. From this we can judge the attitude of the country's leadership towards education.

Education is the foundation of any country. But in our country, the First Education Policy was formulated in 1968, i.e. after 21 years of country's Independence, while the second one in 1986. Implementation of New Education Policy is now under process. After Independence, economic plan is made in the country at regular interval of five years. Annual budgets are made every year at the fixed time. But nothing has been thought so far for making a definite arrangement regarding education.

Whatever commissions or policies regarding education were set up, they gave in some cases good recommendations. But for want of political will, those recommendations were not implemented on ground. For example, in 1968, the Kothari Commission recommended expenditure of 6 per cent of the Gross Domestic Product (GDP) on education, and it was also adopted in the Second Education Policy of 1986. But this has not come in practice until now. Many such examples may be cited to exemplify the government's indifference towards education.

One more important fact is that, after Independence, the government became the centre of all dialogues in the country. **Whereas, in earlier days, society used to be the centre of most of the formal arrangements, including education, in our country.** In the present situation, a general mentality has developed making people in general, and educationists in particular, to think and believe that any reformative change in education is the sole onus of the government. When we talk about education, in my view, these three responsibilities should definitely be fulfilled by the government—(i) they should exact a good education policy, (ii) they should provide necessary infrastructure for education, and (iii) they should aid and support good educationists and good work being done for amelioration of education. But doing ground work in the sphere of education is a prerogative of society, especially people related to education. Society, especially the intellectuals, of that country which begins to depend on government can never witness democracy flourish and succeed in real terms. **American President Abraham Lincoln defined democracy thus—'Democracy is the government of the people, for the people and by the people'. The import of this definition is that democracy can be successful only in that country where administration and related works are run, directly or indirectly, by the people. In a similar way, educational reforms and transformation can be executed and achieved only through the joint efforts of society and government.**

Considering these facts in the backdrop, we have launched our campaign with three basic convictions:

1. If country is to be changed, change education.
2. There can be no alternative of Mother, Motherland and Mother tongue.
3. Talk about solution, not problems.

Essays and articles included in this book are based on the work and experiments being done in the whole country, keeping in mind the basic concept of transformation of education system in the background enumerated above.

Even if we ignore the situation in colonial Bharat, in the post-colonial period too, we have not been able to determine the objective of education. According to Swami Vivekananda, the end of education should be 'man-making and character building'. Same opinion has been expressed by many other thinkers of the country. Essays related to this topic have also been included in this book.

Moreover, many educationists, educational institutions and we have introduced some radical experiments and innovations in schools, colleges and universities with a view to removing flaws and absurdities in education. In the course of these innovations, there have been many novel experiences which were, from time to time, documented as articles and research papers. All such documents have been compiled in this book.

I never, however, feel or believe that opinion expressed in the essays of this book are flawless and absolute truth. **There is no full stop in the journey of thought and development.** On the basis of all these subjects, we have prepared a draft of **New Alternatives in Education.** We are collecting suggestions on this draft through dialogues in the whole country. If readers find some fault in the ideas of this book, or if they wish to give some suggestions to further re-inforce the relevant thoughts, I shall be grateful for communication through e-mail or post.

Prof. Chandkiran Saluja, Shri Rajeshwar, Shri Madan Mohan Sharma and many other persons have directly or indirectly contributed to the preparation of this book, while Shri Dinanath Batra has always given valuable guidance. I express my heartfelt gratitude to all these people. I thank Dr. Vijoy Kant Das for translating the original book into English. And finally, my respectful obeisance to Maa Saraswati, only with whose blessings, this work could be accomplished.

—Atul Kothari

New Delhi

Contents

Educational Change in Bharat: Necessity and Direction

Change in the education system of the country is not merely imperative, rather indispensable. UNESCO's Delors Commission Report (1996) on Education recommended that the nature of a country's education should be consistent with the country's culture as well as its natural growth. Is the shape of education of Bharatvarsh like this? This is the moot question. A poet has painted the perturbing scenario of education in the country in the following lines:

शिक्षा पा कर भिक्षा माँगे, युवजन खाएँ ठोकर आज।
आजादी का स्वप्न दिखाकर, पाखंडी करते हैं राज॥
भ्रष्ट व्यवस्था ने भी, डाला अब यहाँ डेरा है।
चलो जलाएँ दीप वहाँ, जहाँ अभी भी अँधेरा है॥

Educated youth stumble, are compelled to beg,
Imposters cheat with false liberty and rule,
Corrupt system is entrenched all around,
Let's light lamp where darkness still prevails.

A section of society in the country believes that the country is progressing. In some sectors, like Space Technology, Information Technology or Gross Domestic Product (GDP), Economic Growth Rate etc. this appears true. Simultaneously, the number of billionaires is increasing, but poverty and unemployment are also proliferating at the same pace. As its natural result, economic disparity is also widening. Issues like corruption, intolerance, lack of character, decline in morality, blind aping of wrong things of the west, minority appeasement, decline in cultural values, challenge of environment etc. are multiplying day-by-day. Amid such a negative situation, an illusion is being created that the country is developing. Is this attitude acceptable that a small measure of material development means country's total development?

The increase in different types of problems is the result of our wrong policies, confused thinking and negative attitude. From the events taking place in the country and other relevant instances, it appears that the policy of Globalisation imposed in 1990 is proving very nearly unsuccessful. This was imposed on the whole world by America and some developed countries under a conspiracy. The conspiracy boomeranged, and the same countries, including America, are in the grip of dangerous economic slump as an ill-effect of globalisation. America, which was an advocate of no-bar economy, is now obstructing outsourcing in its country from India. Despite such negative consequences, many economists are still advocating globalisation. In the same way, people clamouring against incidence of rape and atrocities on women are, ironically, standing in favour of sexual freedom, homosexuality and live-in relationship. People who habitually criticise the police and governments for deteriorating law and order, criticise any suggestion for infusing moral values and *sanskar* in education, and term it an attempt at saffronisation of the system. Minority appeasement has become synonymous with secularism. They are mostly educated people who support such a vitiated attitude and wrong policies. The main factor that precipitated such a situation in our country is the two hundred year-old Macaulay's education system. We continue to follow it even after 67 years of Independence. Therefore, we believe, 'if country is to be changed, education will have to be changed'.

Regarding education, the Veda says: असतो मा सद्गमय। तमसो

मा ज्योतिर्गमय। मृत्योर्माऽमृतं गमय—i.e., may we be taken from falsity to truth, from darkness (ignorance) to light (knowledge), from death to eternity. In other words, it denotes—सा विद्या या विमुक्तये—i.e., education or knowledge can liberate man from all bonds of life. There should not be any difference between the aim of education and life. From this interpretation, some people begin to doubt that in education, we only talk of spirituality. But this is a wrong presumption. Our root is undeniably spirituality, but our philosophy identifies four human endeavours, in which अर्थ (finance) and काम (coitus/desires) carry equal significance and status as *dharma* (righteousness) and *moksha* (salvation). We have never underestimated the value of *arth* (अर्थ) and kaam (काम), but these, we believe, should be rooted in dharma or righteousness so that our thinking reflects values. If Bharat was not materially rich, why should foreign invaders have to plunder our country? We maintained a balanced attitude towards spiritualism and materialism. Shri Dinanath Batra has termed this attitude, in the modern perspective—'Education for living and life'. It means that education should develop, both, an attitude to lead life, and necessary ability to subsist.

From the facts given above, it naturally emerges that the nature of country's education should be in harmony with our culture, disposition and progression. By education is meant comprehensive development of personality and character building. Education should be an instrument to fulfil national and societal requirements and to address national and international challenges. If this concept of education is to be materialised, it needs to be autonomous and, instead of being commercial, it should be a mode of service. Avoiding any consideration of education in piecemeal, an integrated, undivided circular shape of education has to be conceptualised and, with this at the back of mind, a model of educational family needs to be instituted. With this ancient concept of ours, modernity is to be integrated, while at the same time maintaining an even balance of principle and expediency, a new alternative of education will have to be put forward.

Autonomy of Education

Development of a person, society or nation in the right direction is possible only if it is a free entity. Freedom here means being free from dependence on unwanted things. The central point of principle, practice and policy-making of education is autonomy. Hence, in order to re-establish the real nature of education, it should be completely free from the influence and interference of administration, politics and market. Earlier, when country's education was at the pinnacle of grandeur, it was absolutely autonomous. The Radhakrishnan Commission 1949, Kothari Commission (1966) etc. constituted by the government, have given this recommendation for autonomy. In the same way, thinkers like Kaka Kalelkar, Swami Dayanand Saraswati etc. have expressed their opinion in favour of autonomy to education. In the prevailing administrative structure of the country, Judiciary and Election Commission enjoy autonomy. For both of these institutions, finance and other supporting arrangements are provided by the government, but with the strength of autonomy, various courts have no hesitation in delivering judgements against the government and in favour of the common man. In the recent cases of corruption, notably the 2-G Spectrum Case, the matter could have been hushed up and corrupt politicians would not have gone to jail, if the Supreme Court had not taken cognisance of the offence. We believe that education should be more autonomous than the Judiciary and the Election Commission.

With this purpose, an 'Autonomous Education Council' should be set up at the central level under an Act duly passed by the Parliament. It should have its units at the state and district levels. 'Bharatiya Education Service' should also be organised under its purview. We may begin elaborate deliberations on the texture and the process of constitution of 'Autonomous Education Council'.

Unified Nature of Education

Presently we are deliberating on education in piecemeal. As a consequence, the personality of the youth emerging from this process is divided. This is reflecting in society also. Today's society is fragmented in caste, language, region, rich-poor, man-woman, so-called upper caste—Dalit etc. because at the time of entry of a student to an institution, he is asked about his caste, class and language, which makes him conscious about these.

Our diversity will have to be made a medium of unity rather than one of division. Despite multiplicity of, and differences in, our language, dressing style and food habit, we are one and the same. Our culture, religion, traditions and ancestors are one and the same. We should have a feel of the fact that people following diverse sects and cults are the segments of the same tradition. The texture of the curriculum needs to be devised with a view to creating the mindset of 'one nation—one people—one culture'. The nature of education is expected to meet this end.

Synthesis of the Ancient and the Modern

All that is old is excellent and modern is faulty, or put the old things in the dustbin and adopt what is modern—these are extremist views which should be discarded. We will have to synthesise the ancient and the modern. We will have to contemplate about a new system of education which meets the social requirements, and is rooted in our fundamental principles of education. Sanskrit will have to be synchronised with computer. Computer will have to be included in the learning process, while the medium of one-to-one dialogue will have to be brought in maximum use. While making necessary use of calculator, the value and efficacy of multiplication table should not be underrated. Along with modern mathematics, the value of Vedic mathematics will have to be realised. Seated in an ultra-modern, comfortable building, the sacrosant tradition of teacher-taught relationship will have to be revived.

Educational Family

In the campuses of educational institutions, a disturbing atmosphere of conflict is commonly prevalent these days. Students are against teachers, employees are against administrators, teachers are against management, and so on. For this, teachers, employees and principals have made their unions. This attitude is not compatible with Bharatiya concept of educational campus. No one believes that this school belongs to him, and there is a painful absence of the feeling of educational family. This is the reason behind brewing conflict on the campus among stakeholders. Collectiveness and togetherness cannot be possible without soulful intimacy. In order to develop a healthy atmosphere on the campus, some formal programmes and activities will have to be devised in the beginning. Some programmes like Gurupurnima and Rakshabandhan for strengthening cultural roots, labour-intensive camp, NSS camp, NCC camp need to be organised to inculcate in students a sense of duty towards society and country.

Education: Means of Service, not a Trade

In our country, education has never been treated as a trade. Imparting knowledge has been considered the holiest charity. The arrangement of charging fees from students and paying fixed wages along with DA and HRA to teachers never existed in ancient days. Hence, it did not happen that children of affluent parents would enrol in premier schools while those of poor parents in ordinary schools. There was common opportunity for all. But the commercialisation of education in our times has grown like a monster, vitiating the traditional aura of purity and equity of the schooling system. The relationship between teacher-student is no longer that of mentor-disciple, and has deformed into trader-customer equation. The relation between teacher and management has changed into worker-owner relationship. Teachers have become servants. Admission to premier institutions by dint of money is causing frustration of the meritorious students, who are economically weak. This is aggravating class disparity. Since the time globalisation began, privatisation has been its natural outcome, leading to popular spread of the arithmetic of commercialisation of education.

It is necessary that the responsibility of education should be evenly shouldered by society and government. Government alone running education is not practically possible, but at the same time, this will also be improper that government washes its hands off education completely. The prominent persons of society will have to emulate Shri Azim Premji in this context.

Measures to Improve the Economics of Education Sector

- 6 per cent of the Gross Domestic Product (GDP) should be spent on education.
- At the level of higher education, 20 per cent of the recurring expenditure of traditional courses should be charged from students (as recommended by Puniya Committee), which may be increased to 30 per cent in vocational and professional courses.
- Government cannot be free from the responsibility of providing education. The system should ensure this.
- Fees to be paid by socially and economically backward students should be arranged by government as well as society.
- Meritorious students should never be deprived of education. This must be ensured. A consensual view should be developed that those who are economically well-off should pay higher fees.
- Universities and colleges should explore ways and means to earn from sources other than tuition fee.
- Alumni Associations should be formed and their convention should be organised, through which donors should be identified, who may aid their alma mater.

- Building and infrastructure of the institution can be utilised for raising additional funds.

Recasting Curriculum and Syllabus

While framing syllabus, it needs to be ensured that it is rooted in the past, it is capable of meeting the requirements of the present and, at the same time, keeps in its purview the possibilities of the future. With this view, at the beginning itself, the particular subject's history in Bharat should be taught. There should be a pragmatic agreement between national planning and educational planning. In education in general, and curriculum in particular, there should be a co-ordination of materialism with spiritualism, and of theory with practical. Syllabus should be framed as per regional necessities. It should specially consider the issues of rural and tribal areas. Syllabus should be reviewed every three years. The syllabus should be flexible, not rigid. Syllabus needs to be framed keeping these propositions in the mind.

Presently, a huge imbalance is visible in the courses run in the institutions. For proper planning, it is necessary that a manpower survey should be conducted. This will help to ascertain the number of personnel we need in which sector. On the basis of its findings, required courses should be arranged in related institutions. Currently, a number of absurdities may be seen for want of such a practical planning. In many states, seats in engineering courses are lying vacant. On the other hand, stenographers and computer entry operators of different languages are not available. Pass-outs of post graduate courses of management and of certain branches of engineering stream are finding it difficult to get a job. Even if they get a job, they are not getting status and salary commensurate with their degree. Some time back, a good number of graduates appeared at the interview for recruitment of police constable of a state. The other side of the scene is that skilled tradesmen having no formal education are earning thousands of rupees. Very few courses are available in the country for astrology and

Karmakand (Hindu ritual & ceremony). A lot of hullabaloo is created if a university floats such courses. But there is a great dearth of learned astrologers and knowledgeable pundits (Karmkandis) to perform *samskars* and rituals of various types.

Balance of Theory and Practical

As of now, syllabus is entirely theoretical. The input of practical available at a few places is limited to laboratory. Any system is nowhere in place to gather hands-on experience in field. Former President of Bharat Dr. Abdul Kalam narrated an anecdote: his teacher was teaching astronomy in the classroom; he asked the students if they got the facts; students replied in the negative; then the teacher said that they would meet at the seashore in the evening; in the evening, all met at the seashore; there, the teacher showed to them how birds flew; following this, he asked them if they understood; all the students collectively said—'yes'. In all subjects, practical knowledge is essential to supplement the theoretical one. In compliance of the Supreme Court judgement, environment education is being taught, but in a haphazard way. Hence, it fails to give any positive result, also because it lacks practical approach. In this backdrop, the need of the hour is that environment should be made an integral part of curriculum and it should be taught in the way that while learning it in theory, the learner could also develop a practical attitude. With this purpose, students should be enlightened about air, water, flora, fauna, electricity, foodstuff etc. and how to protect and conserve these as a daily practice. They should be advised to switch off bulbs and fans when they leave their classroom. Along with giving knowledge of science, a scientific attitude should be developed in students. Students should be taught how unhealthy food habit like taking fast food and cold drink, climatically inappropriate clothing, sedentary living etc. are, from scientific point of view, harmful for human health. Unhygienic food material should be strictly banned in the canteens of schools and colleges.

Combination of Science and Spiritualism

This subject is being talked about these days in the whole world. It is being experienced that science fails in explaining the cause of many events taking place in the world. On the other hand, the pace at which science and technology are advancing and expanding, if it is not integrated with spiritualism, it will, instead of development, spell doom of mankind. In this context, the opinion of country's first President, Dr. Rajendra Prasad is relevant:

> "We have not only to preserve the integrity of our nation, but also to keep our cultural traditions eternally alive. The time has come to integrate science with spirituality. This integration alone will give us protection in this nuclear age and orient us towards development."

Teaching of History

Students of the present times are being taught false and distorted history. The kind of history being taught to students for the last 200 years is pushing the self-respect of the country to nought. How we were defeated by the Mughals and the British is prominently taught to students, and with undue emphasis. Contents designed to malign and denigrate our religion, culture, ancient traditions, great persons etc. are served to students. In a book developed by NCERT, it was stated, and taught that Lokmanya Tilak, Chandrashekhar Azad, Bhagat Singh etc. were extremists. Following the prolonged struggle of Shiksha Bachao Andolan, many distorted passages were removed from different books. Instead of teaching only political history, students should be taught history of a period in its totality. The attitude towards history teaching should be such that may arouse in students feelings of pride, esteem and love for the country. Teaching of history should also be such that students could learn lesson from errors committed in the past, lest they recur in future.

Courses of Study should include Resolution of National and

International Challenges. The following issues, among others, need to be included in the courses of study of relevant subjects:

1. Terrorism and National Security.
2. Economic Imperialism and Global Depression.
3. Environmental Hazard.
4. Study of Important Languages of the World.
5. Health Education

Curriculum Should Not be Rigid

Before Independence, the national educational movement had raised the issue of co-ordination of education in the streams of humanities, social sciences, science and technology. It is relevant even today. Presently, one cannot offer as his elective subject, Sanskrit with science, or music with commerce, or economics with science. Many scientists of the world have done diverse research after studying treatises of the ancient Bharat written in Sanskrit. In order to acquire the knowledge embodied in our ancient treatises, one should know Sanskrit. As such, it is imperative that curriculum and subject-specific courses of study are made flexible after removing all rigidity in them.

Social Work

In order to sensitise students about society and to inculcate in them a sense of responsibility as a citizen, it is necessary that hands-on experience of social work should be made a part of curriculum. With this purpose, a commission should be constituted at the national level. Every school should be linked to the slum areas of villages and cities. Today, there are more than 10 lakh schools, more than 33 thousand colleges and more than 600 universities in our country. The number of villages in the country is not more than 5.5 lakh. If one institution adopts one village and works on it, all the villages can be rebuilt and restored to their original glory. Students' involvement in this exercise will inculcate in them sentiment and sense of responsibility for society.

Value-Based Education

In Independent Bharat, all commissions for education, treatises of all sects, cults and religions, apart from great persons of modern times have underlined the requirement of value-based education. **Yogi Aurobindo** felt that since the time education has been divorced from life-values, our countrymen have strayed from righteousness and lost the pious aim of life. Various commissions on education in post-colonial Bharat emphasised the need of value-based education, as given hereunder:

(i) Radhakrishnan Commission 1948-49: According to Radhakrishnan Commission, the Bharatiya view of religion is much the same as secularism *(sarvadharma samabhava)*. In Bharat, the basis of religious education is not possible without spiritualism. Religiosity should be deemed to imply spirituality and, as such, the meaning of religious education should be spiritual education. This commission made some recommendations for moral, religious and spiritual development of students, which are as follows:

- In every educational institution, the students, before teaching is started, should observe silence for a few minutes and practice concentration of mind. Teachers should also participate in this exercise.
- With a view to developing a comparative appreciation of different religions, their treatises like the Gita, the Bible, the Qran, the Gurugranth Sahib, the Dhammapad, the Zend-Avesta etc. should be taught to students in summary form.

(ii) Mudaliar Commission (Secondary Education Commission) 1952-53: Mudaliar Commission recommended that due importance be given in schools to offering collective prayer and narrating inspiring anecdotes to students. The ambience of family, society and school should be conducive to moral and character development of the students. Morality and spirituality should aid students' character-building.

(iii) Kothari Commission (National Development and Education) 1964-66: Kothari Commission recommended that students should be taught about equitable sentiment for all religions *(sarv-dharma sam-bhava)*, as a measure for their moral-spiritual nourishment. Religious education implies moral education inasmuch as students may imbibe positive elements from different religious orders for building their character. Such ideal students are expected to contribute to progression of the country and welfare of humanity.

For value education, separate books are not required. In the syllabus for every subject of the course, moral values should be included. At the very outset, the students of the department should be apprised of the social and national significance as well as relevance of the department concerned. For example, students beginning medical courses should be acquainted with socal and national facts like—that, there are more than 5.5 lakh villages in the country, but a large number of villagers, especially children, die of common ailments because of shortage of doctors in villages; that, this is a big loss of country's manpower, besides being an economic loss. Fresh medical students should also be made aware of, and sensitised about, the fact that medical profession is a mode of service of humanity. Medical students need to be oriented towards their social and national responsibility in a systematic way. If such study material is part of their textbook, students will naturally and effortlessly learn values and ethics. To impart practical knowledge of human values, relevant programmes, activities and project work are also necessary.

Yoga Education

Swami Vivekananda said that if he was reborn as a human being, he would like to study in a school where students are taught how to concentrate, Regular practice of *pranayam*, meditation and yogic exercises improve student's concentration. This will also discipline his life and augment his intellect, which will help him to attain high position in life. Yoga education, therefore, should be an essential part of curriculum. In many countries of the world, the significance of yoga has been recognised, and it has been introduced in the curriculum.

Physical Education and Sports

Healthy students and healthy youth denote healthy life. At present, our country, with 130 crore citizens, is yearning for a single gold medal in the Olympics. On the other side, small children are becoming victims of serious diseases. In order to convert wishes into reality, a strong body is required. To this end, every school should compulsorily include physical education and sports in its curriculum. In addition to this, music and fine art should also be given due space in the curriculum. The knowledge of science and philosophy of ancient Bharat, the valuable heritage of Bharat and the Bharatiya history of the subject concerned should also be included in the curriculum.

Mother Tongue *(Bharatiya Bhasha)*

In pursuit of the cause of educational change, the greatest challenge is the issue of language. This issue should have been settled immediately after Independence, but it could not be done for want of political will. Instead of substituting English with an indigenous language, it was decided to continue English as usual for 15 years. Even after those 15 years, English, instead of having been removed, is gaining strength and influence. After Independence, Gandhiji was once asked to give an interview in English. His reaction was to let the world know that Gandhi did not know English. Mahatma Gandhi, Pandit Madan Mohan Malaviya and many other thinkers have appealed for imparting all our education in our own languages. There is no other country in the world other than Bharat, where primary education is imparted in a foreign language. None in the world has advocated English to be made compulsory. Presidents of America from Bill Clinton to Barack Obama did advise their students to learn mathematics and science attentively, lest students of Bharat and China may defeat them. But they never said this about English. Nonetheless, an illusive atmosphere has been created in our country, in which a person who does not know the 'e' of English, wants his children to be taught in English medium. It is entirely unscientific, illogical and improper. Many studies and surveys have been conducted in the world regarding language whose unanimous conclusion has been that education should be imparted in mother tongue.

Studies of economically developed countries reveal that the medium of their education, public dealing, governance and administration is their indigenous languages. We do not object to learning any language, but we definitely believe and feel that imposing an alien language on 130 crore people is sheer injustice and a callous act of oppression. Those who tolerate such injustice and oppression are as much at fault as its perpetrators. In the given situation, the struggle for right language is certainly difficult, but not impossible. The position of English in the present Bharat is similar to that of French in England 650 years ago. But the people of England, with their will-power, replaced French by English and also became largely successful in establishing English in the world. Therefore, what we need is to arouse an effective will-power.

As a language policy of the country, three-language formula should be adopted. The three languages in this chain are—first, our mother tongue, second, our official language and third, Sanskrit, which is the mother of all languages. The compulsory use of English should be brought to an end at all levels. Once we implement this three-language formula in the country, it will not be difficult to make Hindi and Sanskrit attain the status of global languages. With this end in mind, we will have to begin our efforts from ourselves first. We should do the following things:

1. We should sign in our own language.
2. While writing or speaking in any language, we should use the word 'Bharat' (never India).

3. We should normally use Bharatiya language in our work.
4. We should insist on educating our children in the mother tongue.
5. We and our organisation should produce all the literature in our own language.
6. Translation of books of other languages into Bharatiya languages should be done rapidly.

Research Work

For encouraging research work, expenditure on it will have to be increased. The quality of research work also needs to be improved. Very few of the research works being done in universities are practically utilised in field. Hence, it is needed that research is based on issues relevant to the country and its society. This priority must be fixed for research work. Important facts to be considered in the context of research are as follows:

- Judging the global context, the share of expenditure on Research and Development in Bharat is 2.5 per cent, while that of China is 4 to 9 per cent. (UNESCO—2000).
- In Bharat, research on the topics of pure Sciences are being conducted in small number. This needs to be addressed,. The total share of Bharat in scientific research in the world is just 2.1 per cent, while that of China is 14.7 per cent. (UNESCO—2000).
- Research scholars of the universities of Bharat are being exploited in many ways.
- Research work is being conducted flouting rules, norms and ethics while corrupt practices lead to the award of degree.

Improving the Quality of Teachers

Acharya Vinoba Bhave said that the person who teaches conduct (आचरण) is a mentor (आचार्य). The greatest role in changing education system of a country, and its proper implementation, is that of teachers. It is imperative that 12.5 lakh vacant posts (*Dainik Jagaran*, 2nd August, 2013) of teachers in the schools of our country should be immediately filled up. This too is highly important that proper arrangement should be in place for training the recruited teachers. In the larger context of teacher education, the following measures should also be considered:

- Variety should be introduced in teaching methodology while making suitable changes in it.
- There should be a system or regular training and teacher education.
- Teacher training should include as its subject the elements of moral and professional ethics.
- Modern knowledge should be made available to teachers.
- Skill development and capacity building of teachers should be an essential part of their training.
- Teachers should be made aware of challenges facing the country and society and practical modes to address them should be recommended.
- The notion should be instilled into teachers that teaching is not a profession but a service with a mission.

A group of delegates once visited America for some study, and asked the then President John Kennedy about the reasons of his country's prosperity. His answer was:

'Every student of America has a future. Every teacher in America looks at the President of America.'

Radical change in the system of examination and evaluation is direly needed. Examination and evaluation should be treated as integral part of teaching work. Effective measures should be taken towards conservation, enrichment and strengthening of various types of traditional medical systems and standard courses for them should be introduced.

In order to re-introduce the aforementioned concept of education, it is necessary that citizens of the country are made aware of the value of education through relevant activities. This fact will have to be made popularly acceptable that education is a concern of the whole society, instead of being a responsibility of only the government and some organisations. At the same time, all persons related to education will have to make effective contribution towards implementing 'new alternatives in education'.

For the last 1500-2000 years, such a process of thinking has almost discontinued. This will have to be restarted. This work should be done in every school, college, university and organisation active in the field of education. In this way, the process of extensive change in education will begin. This will ultimately bring positive change in society.

—3 Nov, 2014

□

Commercialisation of Education: A National Challenge

Commercialisation of education is the greatest challenge that the country is facing today. This menace has surfaced in the span of last 40-50 years, but its seeds were sown by Macaulay's educational blue-print imposed on Bharat. Before this, education was never an activity of business or commerce. A friend of mine from Allahabad told me that one of his friends had a hotel, and he also opened a school. His experience was that with a lower investment in a school than in a hotel, higher earning is possible. He closed his hotel and started more educational institutions.

If you desire solution of a problem, you need to fathom out its roots. What is the reason of commercialisation of education and what may be its solution? Some people argue that if education is to be expanded or it has to be made easily accessible to the common man, government initiatives will never suffice. Hence, its privatisation becomes inevitable. Their argument ends at an interrogative logic—why will a person who invests in education and opens schools and colleges, do it without earning profit? Some people step even further and advocate allowing foreign educational institutions in the country to facilitate its expansion and development. Another argument is that in the wake of globalisation, foreign educational institutions cannot be prevented from entering Bharat. All such arguments in favour of commercialisation of education in the country are advanced by the so-called elite of the society.

Condition before Colonisation

Some people have the illusion that education developed and expanded only after the British came to Bharat. In B.C. 700 the Takshashila University (now in Pakistan) was a glorious seat of higher education. Apart from this, Kashi, Nalanda, Vikramshila etc. were prestigious universities in which people from the whole world studied. This is a popularly known and globally accepted fact. Moreover, after a thousand years' struggle (after the British came), the literacy rate of Bharat was 33 per cent (highest in the world) in 1820. The famous Gandhian thinker, Dharmapal, wrote in his book, *'The beautiful Tree'*, that according to a survey done by William Adam, a Christian priest, there were more than one lakh schools in Bihar and Bengal. In Madras Presidency, there was one school in every village. Before 1835, education was the responsibility of society. In those days, kings and affluent persons of society contributed to the functioning of educational institutions without interfering in their management. Later, Village Panchayats also began to support education.

Condition after 1835

During British rule, all indigenous systems of Bharat were gradually demolished. The country's economic condition also went on worsening for this reason. After some time, governmental aid to Sanskrit School was discontinued and that to English schools was raised very high. Students began to be charged fee and grant for funding the school and paying salary to teachers began to be given by the government.

The inevitable consequence of these changes at the hands of the British was that literacy rate, which was 33 per cent in 1820, dropped to 7.2 per cent in 1921. Gandhiji, in his speech at the Royal Institute of International

Affairs, London, on 20th October, 1931, said that during the last 50-100 years, the graph of literacy of Bharat had dropped to an alarming low, and categorically blamed the British for this. At that time, the movement for "national education" was clubbed with Independence Movement. Swami Vivekananda, Swami Dayanand Saraswati, Maharshi Aurobindo, Mahatma Gandhi, Mahamana Madan Mohan Malaviya etc. made valuable contribution to this. As a fruit of these efforts, literacy rate improved to 17 per cent. Before Independence, social organisations like Arya Samaj, Sanatan Dharma Sabha, Bharatiya Vidya Bhavan etc. opened many educational institutions with total dedication to national cause. They never wished to earn from such institutions. Even after Independence, many educational institutes are still functioning with this pious attitude.

Condition after Independence

The entire system of education was taken under government control. Educational institutions were run either directly by the government or through governmental grants-in-aid. The arrangement of charging fees from students, payment of fixed salary to teachers and disbursing recurring grant to run the institution was put in place. With passage of time, a gradual but steady decline set in the governmental educational institutions. Its natural fallout was that privately owned public schools gained popularity. In English medium schools, donation in kind began to be taken. Later on, the malpractices of taking big donation, charging money in teachers' appointment and paying meagre salary to them began. With the gradual fall in the quality of teaching in schools, the practice of giving and taking private tuition gained momentum. Gradually, education acquired the nature and status of business venture.

In the decade of 1960s, a large number of commercial institutes of education were opened in the southern part of Bharat without any governmental aid. In such institutes, big amount of fee—popularly called capitation fee—was charged from students. In a way, these institutes, which were meant for the rich, flourished with elan. A person named Unnikrishnan filed a petition in the court against such institutes. In the contextual judgement, the court ruled that 50 per cent seats should be filled on merit while the rest on capitation fee.

Impact of Globalisation

After 1990, a strong wave of globalisation, also known as liberalisation, privatisation and globalisation (LPG), swept the whole world. It made perceptible impact on the education sector. Governments began to pull their hands off higher education. Initially, vocational institutions stopped being opened by the government. As a result, self-financing vocational institutes began to be opened. Such institutions began assuming different faces like—deemed university, autonomous colleges, private university etc. These are different names for self-financing mode of education. There is no government control on such institutions. In Chhattisgarh, at Raipur, 120 private universities opened in 2002. This was larger in number than that of colleges. The concept of deemed university was modified. Earlier, only institutions specialised in a unique stream of education were granted the status of deemed university, but after modification in provisions, this status began to be given to any private educational institution. This was done by the government itself in connivance with education mafia. Regulatory authorities of the government are dancing to the tunes of the education mafia leading to unbridled malpractices in education sector. Education has obtained a hideous face and educational institutions have debased into vegetable market.

In a similar way, one more provision played an important role in increasing commercialisation of education. Articles 29 and 30 of the Constitution allow minority community to set up educational institutions. But this provision was misused and abused to the extent that institutions with small number of minority students as well as minority teachers and with greater number of members from other community in its management, were granted minority status. Neither government nor court is willing to interfere in this anomalous practice. Petitions were filed against this in different courts of the country. All such cases were clubbed and the Supreme Court heard them. In 2001, the Honourable Supreme Court pronounced their judgement in TMAI Foundation vs. State of Karnataka and Others case. The judgement remained conspicuously silent on minority institution but quashed the earlier order of admitting 50 per cent students on merit in self-financing institutes. The court gave argument implying that it is violative of natural justice to make 50 per cent students (from affluent family) bear the burden of another 50 per cent chosen on merit! While the same court ordered admission of 15 per cent students on merit in Delhi Public School.

The Supreme Court has laid down a new provision for regulating admission and fees in the context of self-financing courses. Accordingly, every state will constitute two committees for admission and fees. This arrangement will be in force until the central or respective state government frames a suitable act. Except Madhya Pradesh, no state has made such an act. Self-financing institutions are charging exorbitant fees in different states in arbitrary way. For example, in some states, fees for engineering colleges are 30 thousand while in some states, these are as much as 70 thousand. Moreover, a certain portion of seats are earmarked as management seats, which are in varying proportion in different states, for which no rates are fixed. Managements are left free to extract from students any amount mutually agreed upon. In this way, lakhs of rupees are being amassed by the management of self-financing institutions. In medical colleges, fees for such seats range from 25 to 50 lakh.

Foreign university is the next ring in the same chain of vicious scheme creating commerce out of education. A parliamentarian asked the Human Resource Development Minister of Bharat if there was a possibility of world level universities like Oxford and Cambridge or professors of such level coming to Bharat. The Minister had no answer to this question. How absurd a thinking is this? Will foreign universities restore the lost glory of our universities? Are we going to unroll red carpet for foreign universities? In all the government, private, self-financing institutions, reservation is applicable. Will it not be applicable to foreign universities? Will there be in such universities, courses to suit our requirements? In all probability, these universities will conduct courses to cater to the needs of multinational companies of their own countries. Their fee-structure will prefer big cities to set up this business. It will be a futile hope that these institutions will foster our cultural values. In an international university of Bengaluru, a teacher taught his students that the traditional family system of Bharat encroaches on your personal liberty. There is a blind attraction in our country for anything foreign or western. Hence, students of our country will not hesitate in seeking admission to these universities paying higher fees, but they are sure to repent before long. In 2002, some students were agitating in Delhi. They approached me for co-operation. Their issue was that they had obtained the degree of MBBS from Russia but in Bharat, they were neither getting a job nor the government was granting them permission for private practice. For such degree-holders, the government had prepared a bridge course of two years' duration. The relevant law provided that getting through this would qualify them to obtain a job or do private practice in the country. These students had got admission to Russian institutes at high fees after obtaining 50-60 per cent mark in qualifying examination. Now they were demanding equity with students with similar degree from native institutes. How can this be possible? I declined any co-operation to them. The way self-financing educational institutions are causing decline in the standard of education and converting education into a mercantile activity, one can clearly foresee that entry of foreign universities will add momentum to its further degeneration.

The prevailing education scenario is one of chaos and disorder. Failure in paying fees is compelling students to commit suicide. To prevent this from happening, parents are forced to adopt wrong means. In fact, commercialised higher education, barring the upper-middle and higher classes, is beyond the reach of the common man. The moot question is whether the children of 80 per cent common people are not meritorious, while those of only 20 per cent affluent ones are? Meritorious students from economically weaker sections of society are facing frustration. Education has not only become a victim of commercialisation, but it has become a highly corrupt business activity. How will students getting education by dint of money construct the nation or give leadership in various sectors? In the given situation, what shape the country's character will take? The hideous face of our country's plight is very much before our eyes today. Characterlessness, corruption and malpractices are rising day by day. Any thinking about these will not yield any result. So long as commercialisation of education is not checked, such problems will continue to increase. The root of all problems of the country lies in education. If country is to be changed, education will have to be changed.

Solution

- Government should enact law to contain commercialisation of education.
- Corruption prevailing in education should be checked.
- Stringent laws should be in place for foreign universities. Their assessment and accreditation should be done both in the country of their origin and Bharat.
- Effective planning should be made for qualitative improvement of educational institutions of the

country, particularly those which are managed by the government.

- Higher education, especially the vocational, should not be left at the mercy of private parties. Government should also mull opening new educational institutions on its own.
- Instead of considering education the sole responsibility of the government, society should gear up to share this responsibility.
- Efforts should be made to revive and re-establish the Bharatiya concept of education.

—27 Dec, 2011

□

Value Education: Status and Direction

If we view the present scenario, we find that Bharat appears to be physically and economically progressing, to some extent, in the areas of space technology, information technology, and some allied fields. On the other hand, evils like corruption, malpractices, depravity, atrocity, violence, robbery are proliferating. We are very much concerned about these, but a suitable solution does not show through. Solutions may be thought about in two terms—immediate and long term. As an immediate step, some evils can be checked through government efforts. For instance, there is much hype in the media about deteriorating law-and-order. This can be improved by imposing strict laws and deploying sufficient police force all around. It is expected that police administration carries out its responsibility efficiently. It is necessary as well. But the common people and the intellectual section of the country is not contemplating seriously about permanent solution of these problems. If we have to think about permanent solution of any problem, the first requirement is to find out the reasons that precipitated them. Problems are actually the results of some causes. The main reason behind the evils or problems under reference is faulty educational system of the country. If the elements of *samskar*, character, morality, spirituality and human value are not essential components of education, how can we expect sane result? The entire world is struggling with such problems. Some countries have economic and material affluence along with reasonable development in science and technology. In many of these countries, there is no bliss of peace, despite the fact that their people are disciplined, patriotic, workaholic and also maintain civic sense. Maharishi Aurobindo said, "Since the time values of life ceased to be a part of education, people of this country deviated from their aim and principle". All thinkers of the country have felt the importance of values of life in education. The treatises of all cults and communities of our country have mentioned it. All the Education Commissions set up after Independence have advocated the teaching of values of life, but it has not yet been included in the formal education system of the country. However, some educational, social and spiritual organisations in the non-governmental sector have tried to include it in their private teaching system under various nomenclature like—moral lessons, spiritual or religious lessons, knowledge of life, human values, life values etc.

The Meaning of Values

- In the context of sale-purchase, the meaning of word 'value' is price or cost.
- The word *moolya* (value) in Hindi emerged from its root form *mool* or root. Therefore, it implies something that exists in its origin or root and also in the tree that develops from that seed. As such, value is the central element of, and intrinsic to, the existence of the tree that a man is.
- Values in a man denote the presence of ideals of life and masculine dignity in him, which can develop his life as a worthy human being.
- Values should include and combine all traits related to the interior (*abhyantar* or *atmanepad*), the exterior (*bahya* or *parasmaipad*) and both together (*ubhayapad*) of a human being.

The Meaning of Education

- Acquisition of knowledge, followed by transfer and training to others.
- *Shiksha* or education has the first place in the six aspects of the Veda (*Shiksha, kalp, nirukta, vyakaran, chhandas and jyotish*)
- In the Invocation section of *Taittireeya Upanishad,* education has been defined thus:

वाङ् मे मनसि प्रतिष्ठिता। मनो मे वाचि प्रतिष्ठितम्।
आविराविर्म एधि। वेदस्य म आणिस्थ: श्रुं तं मे मा प्रहासी
अनेनाधीतेनाहोरात्रन् सन्दधामि। ऋतं वदिष्यामि।
सत्यं वदिष्यामि। तन्मामवतु। तद्धत्कारमवतु। अवतु माम्।
अवतु वत्कारामवतु वक्तारम्। ॐ शांति: शांति: शांति:।

It may be translated as—Let my speech be established in my mind; let my mind be established in my speech; let the knowledge of the self, i.e. manifest *Atma*, grow in me; let my mind and speech be the support to experience the knowledge of the Vedas; let what is heard by me (from the Vedas) be not a mere appearance.... but what is gained by studying day and night be retained. I speak about the Divine Truth, I speak about the Absolute Truth, May that protect me, may that protect the preceptor, may that protect me, may that protect the preceptor, may that protect the preceptor. Ohm, Peace! Peace! Peace!

The above quoted extract signifies that—My voice may be established in my *man* (मन). My *man* (मन) may be established in my voice. You are the Supreme, may manifest or appear at the shrine of education. Whatever education I receive may not go futile or be destroyed. I enrich my day and my night with my study. In my speech, I shall be consistent with religion and justice. I shall speak the truth. That religion and that truth may protect my audience (pupils) and the speaker (teacher)—the interaction between us may be an exchange of ideals. O, the Supreme Soul, the incarnation of *Omkar*! May peace prevail in the three dimensions of the universe—the Earth, the Space and the Inferno.

Other meanings of education are—modesty or obedience and humility. As per traditional wisdom of Bharat—विद्या ददाति विनयम्—meaning thereby, education gives humility.

Significance of Education

- Education should be such that is capable to give proper orientation to the worldly as well as spiritual development of human personality.
- Which should be a carrier of the message of peace for teacher-student, for one's own self and the alien, and for the whole world.
- Which ensures the integrity of thought and speech.
- Which inspires to lead a life consistent with religion, justice and truth.
- Which enables the attainment of Yoga and Security (क्षेम) as well as the material and the spiritual.
- Which makes us humble, polite and soft-spoken.

Three perspectives to understand, Bharatiya values of life

1. Philosophical base.
2. Social consciousness.
3. Personal character or conduct.

In *Guruvani*, it has been said, "Truth is above all things, if anything is above this, it is the conduct rooted in truth".

- Charity (दान), oblation (यज्ञ), meditation (तप), havan (हवन) and Veda (वेद)—all these are based on truth.
- Perception of timeless and immeasurable truth is the highest value of life.
- In Hindu way of life, righteousness (धर्म), materialism (अर्थ), coitus or desire (काम) and salvation (मोक्ष) are

considered four masculine virtues (पुरुषार्थ). The notion of maintaining values of life and righteously pursuing materialism and coitus, is what the Hindu way of life advocates.

- *Manusmriti* identifies ten properties of ***dharma*** or righteousness—*dhriti* (धृति), *kshama* (क्षमा), *dum* (दम), *asteya* (आस्तेय), *shauch* (शौच), *indriya nigrah* (इन्द्रिय निग्रह), *buddhi* (बुद्धि), *Vidya* (विद्या), *satya* (सत्य) and *akrodh* (अक्रोध).

Guru Nanak

- Guru Nanak propounded the philosophy—sing hymns in praise of God, continuously pronounce the name of God and savour holy food in group (संगत, पंगत, लंगर), to promote social harmony.
- The three 'द' sound in consecutive words—दमन (*daman*), दान (daan), दया (daya), mentioned in the *Upanishad* exhorts us to adopt values of life enshrined in these words.

Jain Philosophy

- Jain philosophy emphasises the virtues of truthfulness (सत्य), non-violence (अहिंसा), not to commit theft (आस्तेय) and being non-possessive as well as shunning greed of all types (अपरिग्रह)
- Longing to possess something which is not yours, also amounts to theft.

Shrimad Bhagwat Gita

- One who retains in his possession whatever is left after fulfilling the needs of his living, but does not give it away in charity, then this wealth is like the booty of plunder.

Swami Vivekananda

- As a student, a young man should develop the capacity to prevent the flow of shallow sentimentality in his mind or *man* (मन). For this, he has to be mentally strong and physically well-built with 'rock-like muscles and steely arms'. In such a body dwells a sharp mind that can imbibe all the subtlety of various arts and sciences. Celibacy is the prime requirement of a student for developing strong body and mind

The Message of Shri Krishna in *Shrimad Bhagwat Gita*

- धर्माविरुद्धो भूतेषु कामोऽस्मि भरतर्षभ ॥ 7.11 ॥

  I am the strength of the strong, devoid of attachment and passion and the energy of procreation in all beings, which is not contrary to rightleousness. This is what Shri Krishna says in *Shrimad Bhagwat Gita*.
- *Shrimad Bhagwat Gita* classifies three kinds of asceticism (तप/तपस्या):

  3.2.17.1 Physical asceticism: Reverence for God, scholars and mentors (गुरु), as well as observance of celibacy and non-violence

  3.2.17.2 Asceticism of speech: Speaking the truth, making benign and pleasing statement, and practicing self-study

  3.2.17.3 Mental Asceticism: Positive mind, pleasant thought, modesty, silence, self-discipline.

Pearls of *Sanatan* Wisdom

- The famous saying of *Taittireeya Upanishad* are—one, Mother should be considered as God (मातृदेवो भव), Mentor or Teacher should be considered as God (आचार्यदेवो भव), Guest should be considered as God (अतिथि देवो भव); two, there should be no lethargy in self-study (स्वाध्यायत्मा प्रमदः)

- The journey from self to all, or me to us ('अहम' से 'वयम') is the aim of human life, and that of education too.
- Value-based education lights the path of his journey
- Human body has five aspects—body (शरीर), life (प्राण), mind (मन), intellect (बुद्धि) and soul (आत्मा). Five fundamental values emerge from these aspects—capability, balance, self-control, sensibility and service, respectively.
- The virtues of steadiness (धृति), forgivness (क्षमा), charity (दान), shunning theft (आस्तेय), control of senses (इन्द्रिय निग्रह), intelligence (धी), knowledge (विद्या), truth (सत्य) and not getting enraged (अक्रोध) may be compared to the Ten Commandments for the Jews and Christians enshrined in the Old and New Testaments of the *Bible*.
- *Satyam*, *Shivam* and *Sundaram* represent, respectively, knowledge, desire and action.
- Demon King Prahlad enumerated five primary virtues—modesty (शील), righteousness (धर्म), truth (सत्य), right conduct (सदाचार) and physical strength (सबलता).
- Patanjali advanced eight-fold system for spiritual development and divided human values into two categories—personal and social.
- Consciousness based on values of life was created for people's welfare.
- Noble convictions of the common men of a country in given time and circumstances constitute human values.
- The aim of education is universal welfare of the human being.
- Education should infuse sublimity in the individual.

Speak the Truth. Act Righteously. (सत्यं वद। धर्मं चर।)

- Speak the truth, but righteous conduct is a greater virtue.
- Sharing and empathising with the grief of somebody minimises his grief, and sharing somebody's happiness maximises his pleasure.
- Right aim cannot be achieved through wrong means.
- In our country, we have a traditional notion of adopting strictly righteous means even on the battle ground and to denote this concept, we have a unique word—*dharma-yuddh*, or righteous war.
- Swami Vivekananda had once told an American couple that in their country, a tailor makes a person civilised and cultured, whereas in Bharat, noble and sublime character makes a person cultured.
- Balance or cohesion is another feature of values of Bharatiya life.
- In Bharatiya society, a man of character is more important than a scholarly person.
- So long as righteousness attends materialistic and sensual activities of man, he proceeds smoothly on the proper path of life leading to attainment of salvation or supreme ecstacy.
- An uneducated villager of Bharat may remain ill-fed despite untiring toil, but he cannot abandon his yearning for salvation.
- The natural root of the values of Bharatiya life lies in faith in that unmanifest power—यतोऽभ्युदयानिः श्रेयससिद्धिः स धर्मः, i.e., 'by which comprehensive development may be achieved in all circumstances of life and man may get salvation in life—denotes *dharma* or righteousness.'
- In our land, there are fixed norms for every work and activity, which are popularly considered values of life.
- Materialism and sensual desire are attitudinal values

whereas righteousness and salvation have element of renunciation in them.

- The activities which have the tendency of renunciation, constitute the spinal column of the Bharatiya values of life.
- Religion or righteousness are related mainly to conduct.
- Teaching of values is universally required.
- At present, there is a crisis of character in the world. About the value of character, there is a popular saying:

If wealth is lost, nothing is lost;
If health is lost, something is lost;
If character is lost, everything is lost.

- Without value-education, character cannot be inculcated.
- For teaching values, a separate book is not required. It should, rather, be included in the curriculum.
- *Acharya* (teacher or mentor) comes from *aacharan* (conduct)
- With this view, value-education needs to be necessarily included in the syllabus of teachers' training course.

Evaluation of Value Education

At the first level, learners should be encouraged for self-evaluation of the values of life they have learnt. At the second level, teachers have to evaluate the extent to which learners have been able to imbibe the values of life under targeted value education. Such an evaluation can be done on the basis of students' response and reaction to certain activities, besides other modes. These may be as follows:

- Through continuous and keen observation
- Through students' behaviour in group activities

- Through conversation
- Through the quality of work entrusted to students
- By judging his behaviour in an artificially created situation
- By judging his participation in relief measures during a disaster or natural calamity
- By his interest and participation in sports and games.
- By his interest in books in the library
- By feedback from other teachers and the peerage.
- By his personal hobbies
- Through a written test.

In order to create extensive awareness about the subject of values in the education sector, Shiksha Sanskriti Utthan Nyas is regularly organising seminars, symposia and workshops. Many other educational, social and spiritual organisations are working on value education, giving different name and title to their project. We are striving to bring all such organisations on one platform and to facilitate their collective endeavour in this direction. For education at school level, we have developed the syllabus of 'Teaching of Character Building and Comprehensive Development of Personality'. Based on this, we have developed a book of activities entitled *'Vidyalaya: Gatividhion Ka Aalay'* (विद्यालय: गतिविधियों का आलय). These have been introduced in some schools as experiment. Apart from what has been done for schools, it seems relevant for higher education also. Accordingly, syllabi need to be developed to suit the students of different subjects and faculties. In such syllabi, the basic input will be similar, but certain elements relevant to a specific subject and the profession it leads the student to, should also be considered for inclusion. In the same way, it is imperative that, with due consideration of national requirements, subjects like environment conservation, respect of labour, civil responsibility, patriotism etc. may be added. It is planned to promote and popularise this idea throughout the country. We are also working on inclusion of values in management education. In days to come, we plan to initiate extensive campaign to work on values in the study material of various subjects for their inclusion in their syllabi. We pray that all of us work together to complete this project.

—17 June, 2016

□

Autonomy of Education

The root cause of the distorted form of education in our country evolving presently is that its nature is not compatible with angst, concern and consciousness of the country.

The way a manifest *atma* or the elemental self is called a man, similarly the persons revering essential elements of human existence constitute a nation. From this is created national consciousness. This, in its own turn, creates general consciousness in all aspects of national life. Such a conscious social life is possible only if there exists a pious social milieu facilitating free thinking and free action. In our homeland, all the systems and arrangements were autonomous which made our country developed and flourishing from all angles. There used to be change in governance in different parts of the country, but it hardly affected our national life because all the functional saystems were autonomous. They had autonomous status and existence unaffected by political developments. Society used to run and control all these systems.

A proper development of any person, society and nation is possible only if it enjoys autonomous status. Autonomy means complete freedom from dependence on unwanted things. If the real nature of education is to be revived in our country today, it has to be completely liberated from undue pressures and influence of politics, administration and market.

Once the British left Bharat, education became free from

the shackles of alien interests. At this point began the thought process of Bharatiya educationists towards safeguarding education from falling into the unholy grip of politics. All such people believed that this issue merits serious consideration. In this context, iconic thinkers and educationists as well as educational commissions of post-Independence Bharat also gave their thoughts and suggestions.

Educational thoughts of Kaka Saheb Kalelkar

I am not a housemaid of the government, nor a servant of the law. I am not either a partner of science, or a doorkeeper of arts, or a bond woman of economics. I am the re-advent of righteousness (*dharma*). In true sense, I am the master of man's intellect, senses and the mystic inherent in his being. Anthropology and social science are my twin legs. Art and craft are my two hands. Science is my mind. Righteousness (*dharma*) is my heart. Observation and logic are my pair of eyes. History constitutes my ears. Freedom is my breath. Reverence dwells in my consciousness. I am such a Mother Goddess. My worshipper will never be dependent on any one. All his desires will be fulfilled by my blessings. We have to revive this conception of education.

Kothari Commission's Suggestions for Autonomy

- Departments of the university, its colleges and all their teachers as well as students should get autonomy.
- University should get freedom from pulls and pressures of financing agencies.
- Universities should also be free from the pressure of politics and market.
- Necessary financial assistance must be provided by the government. However, this is also a reason, as some people feel, of the government being able to exert pressure on university. With a view to avoiding this, the audit of the utilisation of government aid should be done by the society, instead of the government.

Suitable rules should be framed to this end.

While ensuring autonomy to the university, its accountability too should be fixed. Its functioning should be transparent so that its autonomy sustains. This is a prerequisite for the university to develop in the right direction and attain pinnacles of educational glory.

Radhakrishan Commission's Recommendations Regarding Autonomy

- Autonomy has vanished due to extraneous pressure.
- University should give due respect to popular feelings. However, functioning under its pressure may corrupt the very system of the university.
- Education should be retained in the Concurrent List of the Constitution. However, the Central Govt. should also see to it that every university maintains minimum standards of excellence.
- Best possible rules and regulations should be framed by learned people for a university. Once it is set up, the government should make it autonomous and abstain from interfering in its work.
- Teachers and students engaged in research activities for ameliorating the standard of education should have functional participation in the governance of the university.
- Rules of the university should not be adverse to the actual perspective of the university. Any anomaly in this context should be removed.
- University should not be made to fit in a pre-fabricated structure of rules and regulations.
- A social group comprising of educationists should govern the university.
- Maximum possible facilities should be extended to students and teachers, ignoring objections, if any, of senior officers.

- University should maintain equitable view of all, which ensures real autonomy.

The Concept of Autonomy

Autonomy is the nucleus of the principle, practice and policy formulation of education. Autonomy is not a separate structure. It reflects the feelings of the society and the nation. Such feelings of the society are co-ordination among elements like unity in diversity, integrated ideals, spiritualism, the attitude of 'all each one' (सर्व खलु इदं ब्रह्म), humanity, tolerance, social cohesion, familial attitude, individual liberty and social discipline. A dynamic system in all the sectors of social life needs to be made the basis of these principles.

In the light of this concept, an Institute for Autonomous Education should be set up at national level to promote autonomy of education.

Institute for Autonomous Education: Its Road Map

- Education should be considered, and pondered over, in totality. Education should be envisaged in its unbroken circular form. Considering education in piecemeal, and in divided aspects separately, will result in the creation of an unbalanced personality of the learner.
- Right from the rituals of conception (*Garbha Samskar*) of the baby to his highest academic attainment, a unified element should permeate the process of education at all stages.
- Ancient knowledge should be modified in the modern perspective, and such modern knowledge should be made nationally popular and acceptable.
- Work should begin for creation of a knowledgeable, spiritual and intensely sensitive society.
- Curriculum, syllabi and textbooks should match the national culture. They should be intended for holistic development of the individual, and for meeting the needs of society as well as the country.

- The aim of education is man-making. From this viewpoint, learner should be made physically sound, feeling-wise balanced, mentally a seeker of truth and spiritually willing to serve.
- With this end in mind, a certain portion of the syllabus covering these ideas and subjects should be common across the country. Some regional variation may be made to suit the specific needs and cultures.
- A comprehensive structure of education needs to be fabricated on the basis of formulae given by educational saint-thinkers like Swami Dayanand, Swami Vivekananda, Maharishi Aurobindo, Bhagini Nivedita, Rabindranath Thakur, Mahatma Gandhi, Dr. Radhakrishnan, Madan Mohan Malaviya etc.

Composition of the Institute

- In order to ensure that the institute may achieve its objectives enumerated above, reputed educationists should be nominated in it.
- Renowned scholars of different sectors of learning should be included in it.
- Along with educationists, teachers, student representatives, chairpersons and directors of educational institutes may be its members.
- The institute should be constituted under a law enacted by the parliament.
- This institute should have an autonomous status greater than that of the Judiciary or the Election Commission.
- Its members should have a tenure of five years.
- Its Chairman should be selected by the President of Bharat through a search committee constituted for the purpose. For final appointment, the President should consult the Union Government and prominent opposition parties.

- Its House of Representatives should comprise of 51 to 101 members. It should have an Executive Council functioning as a core group.
- Its units should be constituted at state and district levels.
- Bharatiya Education Service should be constituted under its aegis.

Functions of the Institute

- The main work of the institute will be to think on providing holistic education. It will be in regulatory, supervisory and directorial role, besides ensuring implementation of its directives.
- To study the main issues plaguing education and to issue directions to educational institutions to resolve them.
- Periodical inspection, evaluation, review and refurbishment of teacher education, curriculum, pedagogy, examination system, admission norms, learner's evaluation and augmentation of quality in education will be its overall responsibility.
- To nominate the Vice Chancellors of Universities, Chairmen of state level Service Commissions and educational administrators at senior positions in various institutes.
- To study the educational set-up of other countries and to create understanding for academic exchange programmes with those countries. Academic programmes may be planned in joint collaboration with such countries.
- To supervise, and be vigilant regarding government, private, government aided and foreign institutions in an even manner.
- To ensure the healthy functioning of the democratic bodies of all types of educational institutions.

Norms for Functioning of the Institute

- Planning should not be one-way. It should, rather, be both top-to-bottom and bottom-to-top.
- The functioning should be fully transparent and corruption-free.
- For redressal of injustice, there should be units of 'Grievance Cell' at all levels.
- Institute's units at district and state levels should be given all powers to function effectively.

A Mindset of Autonomy Should be Created

In Independent Bharat, autonomy of education has always been a topic of discussion because there is a popular perception that our education is in the clutches of government administration. The focal point of such discussion is that the governments of the centre and states are not willing to grant autonomy to education. This is true to a great extent. Nonetheless, this also needs to be assessed if the limited autonomy that is enjoyed by the institutions is being utilised properly. In most of the states of the country, universities are enjoying many types of autonomy. For instance, majority of universities have considerable autonomy in matters of curriculum. But what efforts are being made by them for improving it periodically? How much improvement in curriculum have been effected by colleges which were granted autonomous status by the University Grants Commission? In majority of these autonomous colleges, only arbitrary fees have been levied in the name of autonomy. No improvements in curriculum and examination system are visible in these institutions. Moreover, arbitrary fees are being charged in private colleges and universities too in the shadow of Supreme Court verdict. Such experiences have made a section of society express disapproving view about autonomy of education. On the other side of the case is a pertinent question—are those expecting autonomy from the government, giving autonomy to others? And this is indeed a big question, especially the following:

- Are parents giving their children freedom of choosing courses?
- Are the principals of schools and colleges giving autonomy to their teachers?
- Are the Vice Chancellors giving autonomy to colleges?
- Are the managing committees giving autonomy to their principals?

Another important question that demands our honest answer is highly relevant—is our education free from the undesired influence of market and western notion of education?

If education is to be really made autonomous, it is imperative to consider two-way opinions—from top to bottom and from bottom to top. We need to reinforce our plea for autonomy by exhibiting successful experiments of autonomy at the levels of family, school, college and university. With this purpose, an atmosphere conducive to autonomy will have to be created through small experiments in the sphere of education. We also need to ponder over the issue of autonomy in its totality. Only after this, the education of the country can be truly autonomous.

—4 April, 2009

□

Higher Education: Condition and Direction

In post-Independent Bharat, there has been a reasonable expansion of higher education. Has the higher education of our country been successful in giving to students a right vision of life or in fulfilling their material needs? This is a big and pointed question. Delor's Commission of UNESCO detailed in its report the nature of education of a country as it should be. It recommended that it should be consistent with the country's culture and progression. Does the nature of present-day education of Bharat conform to this? The higher education of the country needs to be conceptualised around its traditional roots and to be moulded according to modern necessities. With this view, suitable curriculum and courses need to be introduced. This draft attempts to make suggestions on the serious issues like enriching research work, augmenting quality of education, making education value-based, making education autonomous and shape of financial management of higher education.

Expansion of Higher Education

Year	University	College	Number of Students	Number of Teachers
1947	18	518	2,28,881	24,000
2009	504	25,951	1,36,42,000	5,85,000

Reorganisation of Curriculum and Courses

- The regimentation of courses needs to be ended.

- Pre-Independence national movement for education had favoured co-ordination among streams of humanities, social sciences, science and technology. This is relevant even today.
- Sensitivity about society and country should be aroused among students.
- Awareness about social and civil responsibilities should be created.
- Social work should be made compulsory for students. Every institution of higher education should adopt a village or urban slum area. A national commission should be constituted to manage and monitor this.
- Our rich cultural heritage, treasure of ancient wisdom and advances in science as well as technology should be made compulsory as a subject at all levels.
- Practical and vocational subjects should be included in courses for students.
- Distortions and falsity included in textbooks and study material that insult and denigrate our culture, tradition, religion and the colossal icons of Bharat should be removed.
- Syllabi should compulsorily be reviewed at the interval of three years.
- Values of life should be included in syllabus.

All the educational commissions of Independent Bharat, all religious cults and sects, and all iconic thinkers have underlined the necessity and efficacy of the suggestions given above.

In course of remodeling and restructuring of courses and syllabi in the light of above-mentioned propositions, the following points must be kept in mind:

- No separate book is required for value education. In the syllabi of all subjects at the level of higher education, lessons on values should be included.
- The social and national significance of learning the subjects of a particular faculty should be made clear to

the learners at the very outset through initial modules of the courses.

- Programmes and activities for imparting practical knowledge to students, commensurate with their level, also need to be included in the course.

Recommendations of Dr. Radhakrishnan Commission for Inclusion of Values in Higher Education

- Teaching of values of life and offering silent prayer should be made compulsory.
- Superb energy of students should be channelised.
- Social work should be a part of the course.
- NCC should be made compulsory.
- Information about our national heritage, ancient Bharatiya attainment of knowledge and advances of ancient Bharat in science and technology should be given to students.

Co-ordination of Science and Spiritualism in the Courses of Science Stream

Of late, a discussion on this notion has begun in right earnest. Many a event has been occurring in the world whose reason and causation could not be explained by science. On the other side, science and technology are developing and expanding at a fast pace. If science and technology are not rationally integrated, they will lead the human being to their doom instead of welfare.

> "We have not only to preserve the integrity of our country, but also to maintain our cultural traditions unto eternity. Now the time has arrived to integrate science with spiritualism. Only this co-ordination will give us, in this nuclear age, the required security to lead us to real development."
>
> —*Dr. Rajendra Prasad*

Some other elements that need to be included in the courses and syllabi at the level of higher education are:

- Teaching of yoga and physical education should be compulsory.
- Sports and games, music and fine arts should be given prominence in the courses.
- All types of distortions and discrepancies, especially those related to history, should be removed at the earliest.

Correct history of the country should be taught to students with a view to stimulating in them a sense of pride for the country, feeling of patriotism and self-esteem. The teaching of history should also be oriented towards inspiring the young learners to learn lessons from mistakes committed in the past and to pledge not to repeat them in future. Students going abroad for higher education should be given special knowledge of our native culture, religion and tradition. Special arrangement should be made for this.

- Course should be framed with two parameters in mind—while being rooted in antiquity, it should meet the requirements of the present and, at the same time, it should have a futuristic vision fused in it.
- In courses, there should be a fusion of materialism with spiritualism and of the ancient with the modern.
- For tackling thc challenges of national and international dimensions, and for fulfilling present-day needs, the following elements should be included in the courses:
  - (i) Terrorism and national security.
  - (ii) Economic imperialism and global recession.
  - (iii) Science with spiritualism and scientific attitude.
  - (iv) Environment.
- There should be a sensible agreement between national planning and educational planning. Courses should be evolved matching the national needs.
- Regional requirements should also be another basis for framing new courses. Rural and tribal area-specific courses should also be framed.

Language

- Study and research in Bharatiya languages should be encouraged.
- Valuable literature of a Bharatiya language should be translated in the remaining languages.
- Only Bharatiya Bhasa should be the medium of instruction in higher education also. English should cease to be compulsory in all types of institutions of higher learning.
- A specialised authority or organisation should be formed to study and publish the manuscripts of Sanskrit.

Autonomy of Education

- With this purpose, an 'Autonomous Education Commission' should be constituted at the national level with its extension upto states and districts. Prof. Yashpal Committee has also recommended formation of national level commission for higher education and research.
- This commission should be constituted on the pattern of Judiciary and the Election Commission. This Commission should comprise, strictly, of educationists.
- The appointment of vice chancellors should be made by this commission, instead of choosing them on political considerations.

> "Educational arrangements should be entirely free from governmental control. Students should be given an uninhibited atmosphere, free from external interference, for pursuit of knowledge. Centres of education should run under the control of society, not government."
>
> —*Vinoba Bhave*

Some Other Important Suggestions for Higher Education

- Super abundant energy of students should be channelised in right direction.
- Higher education should be linked to the needs of

society and country.

- Educational institutions should be opened to meet regional and provincial needs pinpointed by manpower survey.
- Vacant posts of teachers should be filled without any delay.
- Radical changes are required in examination and evaluation system.
- Examination work should be treated a part of teaching.
- Vocational education should be encouraged.
- Bharatiya Education Service should be formed.
- Disparity in education on the basis of religious majority and minority should be stopped forthwith.
- Basic knowledge of Bharatiya history, culture, philosophy and religious cults and sects should be made compulsory for all students.
- Effective measures should be taken for conservation and enrichment of various forms of traditional medical systems. Standardised courses should be introduced for these systems.
- Students' participation should be ensured in the decision-making process.
- Through this participation, students can be made aware of their social responsibility for making them responsible citizens.

If the above-mentioned suggestions are practically implemented, the nature of education thus modified, will make students knowledgeable, adept in skills and crafts and saturated with a natural bent and attitude for service. Such students will be capable of contributing to the fulfilment of social and national needs. They will also be capable of playing a positive role in solving challenges facing the society and the nation.

—10 Feb, 2009

□

Education and Spiritualism

If Bharatiya culture is to be explained in one word, it would be 'Spiritualism'. This is one element that distinguishes us from other cultures and civilisations of the world. It is from this that the following mission-*mantra* (incantation) was born:

सर्वे भवन्तु सुखिनः, सर्वे सन्तु निरामयाः।
सर्वे भद्राणि पश्यन्तु मा कश्चित् दुख भाग्भवेत्।
ॐ शान्तिः शान्तिः शान्तिः॥

Meaning thereby—"May all sentient beings be at peace, may no one suffer from illness. May all see what is auspicious, may no one suffer. Om Peace, Peace, Peace". All our mission-*mantras* or sayings are not sheer principles, but they denote our efforts to make such wisdom emerging from mental and practical experience a part of our life. Later these pieces of wisdom were documented as principles or *shloka* and were enshrined in treatises.

The devil of globalisation imposed on our country is now nothing less than an instrument to plunder the poor and undeveloped countries. But our traditional thesis of '*vasudhaiva kutumbakam*', i.e, 'the whole world is a family' is still visible in practical life and conduct of every Bharatiya individual. This notion enlightened our day-to-day personal, familial, social and national life. We practised these in our everyday activities by giving birdseed to birds, giving flour to ants, mothers reserving the first bread for cows while cooking, before taking food reserving the first morsel for cow, while drawing water from well for our use, giving one bucket to pets etc. For these reasons, Bharat has been acclaimed as a spiritual country.

There was a tradition of giving in charity on special occasions of joy and grief. It was also a tradition to help, with due respect, the poor and the downtrodden. After Independence, the economic condition of the country was bad—it was a phase of utter poverty. There is an inspiring anecdote of that period, about 40-50 years ago. In our village, there were two widows, who had none in the family to support them. In those days, very few women had jobs. About twenty well-to-do families of the village supported them by giving charity to them with due respect. Each family would give them, in succession, food grains, clothing and essential groceries adequate for 15-20 days. In this way, they could meet their ends comfortably and lead their life with honour. Swami Vivekananda had said, "Doing a work with selfless attitude is spirituality. The more unselfish a man is, the more spiritual he is".

Our Upanishads have advanced the concept of righteousness (*dharma*), material possession (*arth*), sensual desire or coitus (*kama*) and salvation (*moksha*). We did not negate or reject *arth* or *kama*, but we did advise their pursuit with *dharma* or reghteousness. A traditional saying explains and exemplifies this—"Earn with hundered hands but donate with thousand hands". We are just the trustees of all that we earn from our trade and commerce. Whatever remains after fulfilling the requirements of our family, belongs to society.

Great persons of the present era tried to adapt them to the modern context. Mahatma Gandhi termed it as 'the Principle of Trusteeship'. In order to apply it in day-to-day life, he called for—'Simple living, Noble thinking'. Different modern thinkers gave a practical shape to this principle. One suggestion was to earmark ten per cent of one's income entirely for the use of society. The iconic thinker of Akhil Bharatiya Vidyarthi Parishad, Prof. Yashwantrao Kelkar, since the very beginning of his career as a teacher, used to spare a certain part of his salary for social work. He followed this vow (*vrata*) till the end of his life.

Even now our spiritual traditions have not ceased to exist. A good number of people are maintaining these virtuous practices in life and society, but, of course, the practice of these traditions has considerably decreased. Earlier, these notions were naturally ingrained in one and all. These may be revived—first, by some practices at home and second, by some input in school. To begin from home, on the occasion of birthday of a child, parents should make them give in charity with their hands and do some plantation. The practices of offering collective prayer with all members of the family and offering birdseed with drinking water should be started. School is a potent means of reviving spiritual attitude. Howsoever adverse the present situation may appear, the school is virtually a place where thousands of students come with an open, receptive mind to learn. Whatever good or bad is taught to them, they are eager to follow. We have introduced the course of 'Character Building and Personality Development' in some institutions through Shiksha Sanskriti Utthan Nyas. In such institutions, some experiments like these have been executed:

(i) In Keshav Vidyalaya and Sharada Vidyalaya of Jhabua (Madhya Pradesh), children offer birdseed and drinking water to birds. Children bring it voluntarily from their homes and collect it in a big pot in school. A natural effect of this is that this practice began in their households as well.

(ii) In a B.Ed. College of Modasa, Gujarat, students and teachers, on their birthday, put their contribution in a charity box kept in the college. Every year, money collected in the box is given away to a good social organisations by way of charity.

(iii) In Swami Vivekananda University of Sagar, Madhya

Pradesh, a course in Disaster Management is conducted. Students of this course are always ready to carry on relief operation in any calamity-struck region, without charging any fees for this.

Many practical experiences like these can be cited as examples. The significance of these experiences is that if children are given such *samskars* in the school, they will spread these bits of goodness to their family and society. In this way, we can easily revive our lost spiritual traditions.

Spiritualism also signifies inculcation of a natural habit to introspect and look inwards in order to 'recognise one's own self'. A catchword of Gayatri Family is—'When we reform ourselves, the world will be reformed'. Now the world has become extrovert and outgoing. Common man to learned people do not hesitate in talking about our Prime Minister and the US President. But they have no time to think and reflect about their own self. And this is the biggest question today.

Man has his own problems and some regarding his family, while society, nation and the world have their separate problems. All look outwards and search for their solution outside themselves. But solution is hardly obtained. Most of these problems originate from man. The solution of the problem exists where it germinated. This is a law of nature. From this view, the solution of all our problems is available within ourself. All the great persons of the country and the world who made positive contribution in any sphere, must have had the habit of looking inwards. By dint of this habit, they could give solution to problems of the society. Development of such a vision in man is itself spiritualism. Looking inwards means getting close to one's soul. Our basic form is soul, and soul is a fragment of the Divine soul or supreme power. The more a man gets close to the soul, happier and blessed he becomes. This has been conceptualised in the *Taittiriya Upanishad* as *Panchkosh*, of which the last one is the *Anandmaya Kosh*. Here *'Anandmay'* denotes spiritual development. Only a spiritual individual can experience true ecstasy.

The meaning of '*aadhyatmik* ' (आध्यात्मिक or spiritual) is *aadh* + *aatmik* (आ+अधि+आत्मिक), i.e., journey to the inner self. By spiritual nature of education it is meant that courses and curriculum should be intended for arousing in learners selflessness and attitude of service. To achieve this, suitable activities should be introduced in schools. Shiksha Sanskriti Utthan Nyas has prepared syllabus for Environmental Awareness for classes I to XII. In this syllabus, every lesson begins with *Shloka* regarding environment, which have been taken from ancient Sanskrit treatises. The meaning of all such *shlokas* are also given. Our ancient treatises must be read for developing environmental awareness because our ancient saints were conscious about its relevance for mankind some thousand years ago, whereas the contemporary concern about this is hardly 100 years old. The unmistakable purport of this fact is that the Bharatiya attitude has been highly proactive. We believe in envisaging a future problem and devise ways and means to prevent it from occurring. On the other hand, the western attitude is to initiate measures to solve a problem only after it occurs. Allopathic medical system is a living example of such a western attitude. Our Ayurvedic medical system provides effective preventives for diseases likely to appear in future. For making students proactive about environmental problems, we have appended to lessons some relevant activities to be done by them. After learning what the teacher has taught, and after the teacher has done the teaching, both students and teachers have to decide what they have to do in their personal, familial and social life. Developing such an outlook is the spiritual view of the curriculum. The nature of education should, in entirety, be like this. Shiksha Sanskriti Utthan Nyas is striving in this direction with firm determination.

—16 May, 2018

□

Character Building and Holistic Development of Personality

To enable a man to express his inherent perfection, experience that boundless potential as well as holistic development, while building his character, is the aim and purpose of education. Our ancient treatises as well as modern thinkers like Swami Vivekananda, Bhagini Nivedita, Maharishi Aurobindo, Rabindranath Thakur, Pandit Madan Mohan Malaviya, Mahatma Gandhi etc. have articulated the same notion matching the prevailing situation of their time and clime.

Bharatiya Thinkers on Education

Mahatma Gandhi: My notion of education deems it an act to manifest the noble elements existing in a child's or man's body, mind and inner self (*atma*), and to facilitate its multi-dimensional evolution.

Mahamana Pandit Madan Mohan Malaviya: He considered education as a means for all-round development of human life. In his view, 'education is that instrument which can enrich and foster a student's physical, mental and emotional development'. In the opinion of Mahamana, evolution of character is the end of education.

Bhagini Nivedita: We should be workaholic and energetic while being dedicated to the service of mankind. Development of an active, zealous and tenacious personality of students should be the objective of education. The aim of education is not merely earning a livelihood, but its aim should be character building, personality development and nation building.

Swami Vivekananda: The total nature or character of a person is known as his personality. Education is not an accumulation of diverse information which has been stuffed in your mind. It remains there without getting assimilated the whole life and creates incessant commotion. In my view, the quintessence of education is not stockpiling of facts, but to develop concentration of mind. We need such an education which builds character, nourishes mental strength, augments wisdom and, above all, enables man to stand on his own feet without any support. Put in a different way, 'we need an education which creates 'man' suitable in all walks of life'. Swamiji says that 'one and the only aim of education and learning is sculpting a man'.

Maharishi Aurobindo: In a fair and just social order, every individual will get equal opportunity, every individual will be given common education for nourishing his mental faculties and putting them to use, so that man may realise the dignity of his entirely emancipated inner self. This will facilitate man to work with his full capacity.

Rabindranath Thakur: Man is full of boundless creative power. Being an integral part of nature, he is essentially pious and multi-dimensional. He is to be made aware of this. Education is the best means to this end.

The concept of *Panchkosh* (पंचकोश) propounded in *Taittiriya Upanishad* meant for comprehensive development of personality leads to actual perfection.

The Concept of Personality

Man is the manifest form of the elemental self (*atmatatva*). In this cosmos, the supreme manifest form of beings is Man. The abstract nomenclature of 'Person' is 'Personality'. A person has two aspects—material mass and subtle substance. His physical frame is the material mass. His *prana, buddhi, man* and *atma* are subtle substances. To know the personality of man amounts to becoming aware of *panchkosh* and to develop it in entirety.

Panchkosh

1. Annamaya Kosh – Physical development
2. Pranmaya Kosh – Development of *Prana*
3. Manomaya Kosh – Development of *man*
4. Vigyanmaya Kosh – Mental development
5. Anandmaya Kosh – Spiritual development

Annamaya Kosh

Our body is *Annamaya Kosh*. It is nourished by grains, therefore it is called *Annamaya Kosh*. Body has two parts. One is external body and the other is internal body. The organs like hands, legs, ears, eyes, nose etc. which are visible outside are external body. Our digestive system, respiratory system, circulatory system etc., which are hidden under the cover of skin, constitute our internal body. Our body is physical manifestation of our being. Human body is an apparatus. All the limbs and organs of the body are its functional tools which perform diverse tasks. In order to understand our body, we should understand (i) the design and composition of all limbs and organs of the body, (ii) their functional role, (iii) their modus operandi or way of functioning (iv) how these are looked after, how these are nourished, and what to do to keep them healthy. Very little information regarding these is given in our educational system. In courses of only science stream, some information is included. But knowledge of these is necessary to be given to students of all streams in orderly manner.

When the body is sturdy, energetic, flexible, shapely and free from disease, the body may be considered healthy, and *Annamaya Kosh* may be said to be in proper shape. The way food, sleep, exercise, sports, yoga, regular activity and maintenance of daily physical labour also impact our health positively. With this purpose, we should ensure the following measures in our schools:

- Students should be informed about the biological composition of human body, and functions of its various limbs.
- Provide at least 20 minutes' period each day for physical exercise.
- Students should be apprised of scientific approach to food habits.
- Junk food, fast food and cold drinks should be avoided in canteens.
- Every student should participate in at least one game.
- Comprehensive health check-up of every student should be arranged at least once in a year.
- Students, teachers and principals should collectively conduct weekly cleanliness campaign on the campus.
- Organising labour intensive camps in the school through NSS.
- For environmental conservation, necessary steps should be taken in the schools. Besides, students should be inspired to include practical life measures for enrichment and conservation of environment.

Pranamaya Kosh

The force or energy that operates the body is *prana*. Something which has no *prana* is inanimate whereas something which has *prana* is animate. The part of that body in which *prana* does not circulate, becomes inactive. *Prana* is life-force. *Prana* is subtler than body, and it pervades the whole body. *Prana* cannot be seen, but it can be only experienced. The way electrical energy cannot circulate without a conductor, *prana* also circulates through the medium of breath. Hence we need clean air to breathe. By clean air is meant the air that contains about 21 per cent Oxygen, also known as life-breath (*prana-vayu*). Hence, it is imperative that environment is clean. With proper development of *prana*, man enjoys good health and longevity. For development of *prana*, *pranayam* is the best medium.

Prana has four impulses—food, sleep, fear and coitus. These are four essential and vital stimuli to hold *prana*. Human body is an apparatus which needs to be made functional. The impetus of *prana* makes it functional. Human body may be likened to a motor car which has wheels, engine, steering wheels, doors and driver but it needs fuel to run. As such, students need to be inspired to develop *prana* in the following way:

- Students should be made to practice yoga and *pranayam* regularly.
- Students should be given a thorough understanding of factors creating imbalance in the *prana*. Some of these factors are:
  - (i) If one does something wrong, the *prana* is unbalanced. For example, telling lies, being envious and being angry with someone disturb the balance of *prana*.
  - (ii) Ill health also causes imbalance of *prana*.
  - (iii) Doing a work in hot haste also leads to imbalance of *prana*.

Manomaya Kosh

Manomaya Kosh is related to *man* (मन). It is a very important *kosh. Manomaya kosh* is positioned at the centre of the series of five *koshas*—two before it and two after it. *Man* is subtler than *prana*. *Man* does not need any support. *Man* desires, it may be contradictory and ambiguous. *Man* has the conflict of the contraries like taste and distaste, pleasure and pain, love and hatred, happiness and distress, resolution and options. *Man* considers and contemplates. It converts all types of stimuli received from the senses into thought. Such thoughts later get the tinge of pleasure or pain etc. *Man* is excited but it can concentrate. *Man* is addicted to the subjects of its taste. *Man* is disturbed, excited and tense but it can also be at peace. *Man* has the highest speed in the whole universe. *Man* is also very powerful and it is hard to be tamed. To make *man* calm, concentrated, detached and free from conflict means development of man.

Man is like water. In the same way as rainwater does not have to make any effort to merge with water of river and ocean, *man* also need not make any special efforts to decline downwards. If we have to make rainwater flow in our wash-basin, we have to devise ways and means for this; in the same way, in order to make *man* upwardly mobile, we have to make special efforts with due diligence. *Man* has in it positive instincts like pity, kindness, love, sympathy, compassion etc. while it also has in it evils like greed, attachment, pride, envy, carnal desires, anger etc. To enhance positive instincts, and to curb evil ones, means the development of *man*. Self-study, sane company, service, music and yoga keep *man* in proper shape. Restraint, good conduct and virtue make a healthy *man*. *Man* influences body, and the vice versa. So long as *man* is not healthy, *buddhi* or sensibility does not function properly. It has been rightly said— मन चंगा तो कठौती में गंगा, i.e, if your mind is pure and healthy, the water in your bowl is as pure and pious as that of the Ganga. The following input is recommended for students:

- Specific activities for students for making *man* stable, concentrated and free from tension.
- Specific activities for giving positive direction to *man*.
- *Man* has a strong impulse of attachment, which needs to be oriented towards detachment.
- Music, self-study, service and good company are blessing for development of *man* in the direction as above.

Vigyanmaya Kosh

The function of *buddhi* (intellect) is to know. From this view, *buddhi* is related to knowledge. The expansion or extension of knowledge is *vigyan*. As such *Vigyanmaya Kosh* signifies intellectual development. Intellect, with the help of the intellectual senses does observation, scrutiny, analysis, synthesis, logic and through hypothesis, discerns right and wrong—this is called prudence (*vivek*). On the basis of prudence alone, *man* takes just and proper decision. This is the principal function of intellect.

Intellect to use its prudence and judgement properly to requires *man* to be healthy. In the *Mahabharat*, Duryodhan had said— जानामि धर्मं न च मे प्रवृत्ति, जानाम्यधर्मं न च मे निवृत्तिः—it means: 'I know what *dharma* (righteousness) is, yet I cannot get myself to follow it, I know what *adharma* (vice) is, yet I cannot retire or refrain from it'. This shows a conflict between *man* and *buddhi*. When *man* is not healthy, such a situation surfaces.

Nowadays, science is taught in most of the institutions but scientific attitude does not develop in students. Scientific attitude denotes comprehending something in the right perspective and to work and behave accordant to this. In order to develop the *Vigyanmay Kosh* of students, it is imperative that their *man* attains proper health, they develop inquisitive tendency, they become prudent and they inculcate the habit of self-study. To ensure that their development follows this line, it is required that their text of study is textured on that pattern, competition is organised in co-curricular activities and teaching methods should be developed and adopted to inculcate an attitude of inquisitiveness in students.

Some specific inputs in teaching as mentioned below may help to develop *Vigyanmaya Kosh* in young learners:

- To develop scientific attitude, students should be made to practice suitable activities.
- To demonstrate and make students practice scientific modes of decision-making.
- To train students in general awareness, art of expression and presentation, art of writing and various fine arts, besides holding competition in all skills.

Anandmaya Kosh

Anandmaya Kosh signifies spiritual development. Some scholars term it psychic (*atmik*) development or moral development. Being spiritual means 'आत्मनो मोक्षार्थम् जगत हिताय च' or 'to work for one's own salvation and welfare of the world'. With this view, Swami Vivekananda said, "Doing any work with a selfless attitude is spiritualism". This statement means well-being of the world. The notion of आत्मनो मोक्षार्थम्, or 'salvation of the soul', requires that man should become introvert, as a first step towards it. Majority of people have become extrovert nowadays. As a man gradually becomes introvert, he gets closer to the soul (*atma*). Human soul is a part of the supreme soul (*parmatma*). It signifies that getting close to the soul is like getting close to the supreme soul (*parmatma*). This will lead to the ecstasy of knowing, understanding and realising one's own self.

For spiritual development of students, teaching in school should aim at inculcating in them attitude of service through organisation of suitable programmes and activities. Simple activities like offering birdseed, serving slum areas or village folk will go a long way in their spiritual development. To develop spiritual tendency and to make them introvert, curriculum and teaching method should be suitably modified. The following activities may prove useful:

- Students should be encouraged to offer charity on their birthday, to do plantation work, to give birdseed and drinking water to birds. Through these activities, children will develop naturally and effortlessly, the disposition of service.
- Students should be trained to look inwards and made capable of doing positive introspection. The nature and contents of the textbooks should be designed to make students sombre, thoughtful and introvert.
- Students should be regularly taken to villages and

slum areas of cities to give them a firsthand experience of life in utter poverty.

A balanced growth and enrichment of all the *koshas* from the *Annamaya* to the *Vigyanmaya*, paves the way for ideal development of the *Anandmaya Kosh*. It is, therefore, imperative that proper care should be taken to nourish all the five *koshas* in every student, which will lead to their elemental pleasure.

Development of *Panchkosh* will naturally make students physically sound, lifewise balanced, mentally positive, intellectually rational and spiritually service-oriented. From this perspective, development of personality is a process while a finely built character is its natural fruit. Students with their personality developed on this pattern and endowed with high character are capable of making a nation and working for the welfare of humanity.

This article enumerates the theoretical aspects of the *Panchkosh*. Based on these principles, Shiksha Sanskriti Utthan Nyas has developed syllabus for 'Personality Development and Character Building'. The schools, colleges and universities which introduced this course in their institution and made determined efforts to implement them, have experienced phenomenal results.

—7 Aug, 2019

□

Education for Social and Human Health: An Alternative Design

In the recent past, the Union Government proposed a course in Sex Education, which was rejected by the majority of groups. Compelled by adverse reaction of the society, the government withdrew this perverted plan. CBSE has presented a new model on its website. Hence, we also decided to frame an alternative design of education based on the Bharatiya concept of human psychology. Now it is taking a tangible shape. Sex is a natural and spontaneous process which requires no formal instruction. Human body is afflicted with a disease in one of these conditions—one, when the body is weak and two, when we did not take care of a healthy body. In the same way, evil creeps into man's mind and thought in one of these situations—one, when social atmosphere is polluted and two, when the mind (*man*) is healthy but we did not care for it.

Human weakness are of two types—internal and external.

Causes of Internal Weakness

- Personality has not been developed in entirety.
- There is insufficient dialogue in the family. Queries in the mind must be answered.
- Lack of pristine love and intimacy.

Causes of External Weakness

- Too much openness in society and blind imitation of the west.

- Some serials and indecent advertisements shown on television and indecent literature circulating on internet.
- Sexual abuse of youngsters by other people.
- Problems typical of children from too rich or too poor families.
- Lack of pristine love and intimacy in the general atmosphere of the family.
- Absence of suitable instruction through dialogue with family.
- Lack of comprehensive development of students' personality.
- Lack of required efforts for maintaining mental health of students in the past. The present situation demands huge efforts for its correction.

Comprehensive Development of Personality

"The function of education is just to make perceptible the noble perfection latent in man"

—*Swami Vivekananda*

"The aim of education is to accomplish the task of developing to the maximum the beauty and perfection of human body and soul."

—*Pluto*

The Upanishad and the Concept of *Panchkosh* for Personality Development

1. **Annamaya Kosh:** In order to maintain human anatomy in good health, physical exercise, sports, yoga, plain (*satvik*) food, adherence to fixed routine, cleanliness and continence are required.
2. **Pranamaya Kosh:** Yoga and Pranayam, practice of yogic *yam* and *niyam*, concentration of mind and offering prayer nourish this Kosh.

3. **Manomaya Kosh:** Self-study, good company, music and poetry, creative tendency, being disciplined and organised, execution of duties while remaining conscious of one's rights, social equity and cohesion promote enrichment of this Kosh.
4. **Vigyanmaya Kosh:** It signifies increasing virtues and enhancing the range of knowledge. Dialogue, inquisitiveness and its resolution, resolution of problems, co-ordination, being sensible and responsible, sense of mutuality, alertness, capacity of appraisal, viewing inwards to observe one's own self, soft-spoken, meditation, sense of cosmic elements (*tatva-bodh*), search of truth and creative tendency promote the health of Vigyanmaya Kosh.
5. **Anandmaya Kosh:** Service, social work, sharing collective responsibility, being compassionate, dedication, concentration and meditation, gratefulness, devotion to duty and stress-free life enrich this Kosh.

Man attains holistic development when his thoughts are grounded in the *Saptapadi*. The seven elements of the Saptapadi are:

- Individual—person and personality
- Family—mutual compatibility and intimacy
- Society—social cohesion
- Nation—indivisibility of the nation
- World—welfare of the whole world
- Cosmos—unification of soul with the supreme soul

□

Environmental Conservation and Sustainable Development in Education

Man is a unique gift of nature. Being a thoughtful creature, man has the greatest responsibility regarding nature. If we talk of the greatest danger at global level, problem of environment and the menace of climatic change have emerged as the most serious one. Education *sanskarises* a raw human being by making him aware of his natural responsibilities. Only if environmental conservation and sustainable development are evenly introduced in the curriculum, we can overcome the environmental menace.

UNESCO, in its Delors Committee Report, said that education of a country should be compatible with its culture and progression. I have added one word to this—'nature'. Is the present-day education system of Bharat consistent with its nature, culture and progression? This is a crucial question. We should have such an education as we wish to make our country, our society and our citizens. Education constitutes the foundation of a country.

If the country and the world needs sustainable development, our education should be accordant to this. The world is facing two major problems—(1) Terrorism (2) Environmental Pollution. Sustainable development is related to environment. Today the world is standing at the crossroads. A common notion has developed that any attempt at environmental conservation is detrimental to material development. With any increase in material development, environmental imbalance also increases. A practical, pragmatic and balanced co-ordination between the two only may result in sustainable development.

Efforts Made at Global Level

United Nations Development Programme (UNDP) in 'The 2030 Agenda for Sustainable Development' says—"We should acquire necessary skill and knowledge to promote sustainable development through education". United Nations Organisation (UNO) observed the Decade of Education for Sustainable Development (DESD) from 2005 to 2014. From this emerged the notion of Green School. This was launched in Europe in 1992. In the Earth summit at Rio in 1992, its need was underlined. Efforts on this line gained momentum with World Summit of Sustainable Development (WSSD) held at Johannesburg in 2002.

Green School

Green School is seen as an institution that has been conceptualised through the principles of sustainability. It builds on environment for co-ordination of all the resources and opportunities available within and outside the school for sustainable development. This, at the next step, sensitises students and teachers for participating in the direct action of the community on this front. This is not just a one-time action. Rather, it demands continuous action for correction in environment by the beneficiaries in schools and adjacent areas.

In such an atmosphere, the learning experience of students does not remain limited to the classroom but it transcends to other spheres of their activities. These local resources are meant for children which are used for giving direct experience to them. These experiences help them to acquire knowledge, to do an experiment, to promote the tendencies and inter-relation among environmental processes, to develop an understanding of environment in children, to inculcate values in children and to make them compassionate. Such an education may be termed holistic, capable of ensuring total development of children because it includes in its structure the informal resources available within and outside the boundaries of the school.

Efforts Made in Bharat

In Bharat, National Committee on Environmental Planning and Coordination was set up in 1972. In 1988, National Forest Policy was launched. In the Kothari Commission (1964) and New Education Policy—1986, deep concern was expressed regarding the menace to environment. In the NCERT curriculum of 1975, 1988, 2000 and 2005, environment was incorporated as a subject. In Article 15(A) of the Bharatiya Constitution, the conservation and enrichment of nature, environment, water, forest, wildlife etc. have been termed one of the fundamental duties of the citizens. The Article 48(A) of the Bharatiya Constitution identifies conservation and enrichment of forests and wildlife as one of the Directive Principles for the state. On 18th December, 2003, the Supreme Court made it mandatory to teach environment as a subject at all levels. For many decades in the past, efforts are underway at national and international levels, for conservation of environment. The UNESCO sponsored Education for Sustainable Development Decade completed its period three years back, but the problem of environment, especially global warming, keeps increasing.

If you wish to solve a problem, you have to penetrate to its roots. The root cause of this problem, to my mind, is 'epicurean lifestyle'. In most of the lines of thinking, including the western one, nature has been considered a source and means of enjoyment. In the traditional thought of Bharat, nature has been given the status of mother. But it is unfortunate that for the last few years, we have deviated from the path recommended by Bharatiya thinkers. Mahatma Gandhi had said, "Nature can fulfil the needs of man, but it cannot fulfil his greeds."

For addressing environmental issues, syllabus rooted in Bharatiya thoughts needs to be developed. From this view, Shiksha Sanskriti Utthan Nyas has made the syllabus for environmental education. Every lesson begins with the Bharatiya notion of environment. The lessons of the study plan open with relevant mantras, hymns and psalms of ancient Bharatiya treatises, and their meanings have been explained.

What, after all, is the justification of attaching so much importance to Bharatiya thoughts on environment? The present menace to environment is a result of the notion of material and industrial development prevailing over a period of around two hundred years. But the mantras about environmental conservation in the ancient Bharatiya treatises were composed some two to five thousand years ago. No such problem existed then, but they could envisage its possibility in future. Hence they were proactive. They suggested ways and means to protect environment. Hence it is wise to take steps to restrict the problem from precipitating instead of groping for solution when the problem arises. In the western and European thoughts of the ancient times, there are few thoughts on environment. This makes Bharatiya thoughts on environment highly relevant in the global context.

In 1992, the then Prime Minister, P. V. Narasimha Rao, speaking at an international conference on environment, said that if the world wishes to get a solution to this problem, it will have to come to Bharat. A child of our home, just after he wakes up, before placing his foot on ground, chants this mantra keeping his palms unfolded:

समुद्रवसने देवि! पर्वतस्तनमण्डले।
विष्णुपत्नि नमस्तुभ्यं पादस्पर्शं क्षमस्वमे॥

It means—"Oh Mother Earth, O Devi, you who have the Ocean as your garments, and mountains as your bosom. O consort of Lord Vishnu, salutations to you, please forgive my touch of the feet on earth which is your holy body". After this, the child cleans and washes his body, puts on clean clothes and gets ready for his routine morning prayer.

The educational institutions which followed our syllabus on environment with due determination have reaped phenomenal results. Our syllabus lists some activities at the end of every lesson. Once the teacher teaches and students learn, teachers and students are inspired to think how the matter taught and learnt in classroom may be translated into practice in their personal, familial and social life. Developing a vision like this through education means spiritual vision. This too is the Bharatiya vision of education for sustainable development.

Contemporary society has become extrovert. People cannot look inwards to find out the causes for, and solution to these problems in their inner self. They have developed a habit to look outward upto the government and other systems for solution. They never introspect on their role in causing or solving the problem. Very few people tend to think about their own role in it. This is the prime reason for family, society, nation and the world not getting solution to its problems. A suitable correction in our personal attitude is direly needed.

—7 Oct, 2009

□

Relevance of Bharatiya Tradition of Thought and Wisdom

Inclusion of Bharatiya tradition of thought and wisdom in the syllabus of environment in technical education stream not only creates awareness about the sublime nature of Bharatiya tradition of thought and wisdom, but also throws light on the logical solution to environmental problems in the context of contemporary needs. A popular question is—why is Bharatiya tradition of thought and wisdom needed to be included in formal education? The answer is—because the fundamental knowledge of Bharat is perfectly scientific.

The menace to environment is not one of Bharat alone, but of the whole world. Dialogue on environmental hazard began at global level in 1972. The United Nations Organisation decided in 1972 to observe Environment Day every year. It was observed, however, in 1974 for the first time. Actual problem must have arisen some years earlier. But why Bharatiya saints and thinkers hundreds and thousands years earlier wrote in their treatises mantras and maxims about environment conservation? From this, I am inclined to conclude that the western attitude is one of finding a solution after the problem appears. Whereas the Bharaitya attitude is being proactive so that the problem fails to surface. As such, the traditional knowledge of Bharat in ancient treatises is capable of providing solution to most of the problems facing the world. This truth is being gradually accepted by the world

International Day of Yoga was internationally accepted with near unanimity and it is being observed every year. It testifies the acceptance of a luminous gem of our traditional knowledge. This also substantiates the facts that yoga has the potential of preventing and curing many ailments for which European medical system has no effective method. The world accepted Yoga because of its efficacy. The thoughts of ancient saints of Bharat are rooted in scientific ratiocination. For this reason, many Islamic countries have also adopted yoga. An equally valuable scientific knowledge of ancient Bharat is Ayurvedic medical system. Unfortunately, we have not been able to develop it to the required extent. When we accomplish this with regard to Ayurveda, this system will have greater acceptability than yoga in the whole world. We expect this because Ayurveda is capable of both preventing and curing diseases with which the whole world is ailing without positive solution at hand.

We talk of Bharatiya tradition of knowledge instead of ancient knowledge. Bharatiya tradition of knowledge, as a nomenclature, embodies and expresses greater significance as it incorporates in it the ancient, the modern and the modifications over the passage of time. The ancient knowledge is simply excellent, but the thought process unleashed by it is a perennial flow, which is alive even today. Its force, however, has slowed down. But the saints and thinkers of the last two hundred years, like Swami Vivekananda, Maharishi Aurobindo, Jagdish Chandra Bose, Prafulla Chandra Roy, Shrinivasa Ramanujan etc. led forward the chain of thoughts of Bharatiya tradition itself. The knowledge these thinkers gave also constitute a part of Bharatiya tradition of knowledge. The massive flow of thoughts emerging from the Vedas, the Upanishads and all other noble saints and thinkers is the traditional Bharatiya knowledge.

The intermediary period of one thousand years or more between the period of native rulers of ancient Bharat and the end of British colonialism, the country was tormented by continual foreign invasions leading to disruption of the natural flow of the tradition of Bharatiya knowledge. But the trail of thought never ended completely. Now that we are a free country for the last 73 years, the onus falls on academicians, scientists, social and political leadership etc. to revive and add momentum to the tradition of Bharatiya knowledge. There is no dearth of talent and genius in our country. The whole world recognises the merit of Bharatiya students. Our students are supposed to be at the top in the whole world in respect of intellectual brilliance. In order to promote such a talent, we need to think over some basic facts.

The first important thing is that the educational system of Bharat requires drastic transformation. In the present system, only some stereotyped theoretical knowledge is given to students. For years together such a mode has been continuing in most of the institutions. There is a total lack of pragmatic attitude in the way knowledge is transferred. So long as the method of teaching and learning is not suitably modified, students cannot achieve much even after graduation. Mahatma Gandhi advised harmony of head, hand and heart, ie, *gyanayoga*, *karmayoga* and *bhaktiyoga* as laid down in the Gita. It signifies that if one works with hands and learns through mind with an even input of feelings, only then a sensible student is forged. The same notion was put forth by the Delors Committee in these words—"Learning to know, learning to do, learning to be and learning to live together."

The second important matter is that until education is given through mother tongue, a really knowledgeable society cannot be built. It is not a mere emotional idea, but a virtual scientific truth. Even the syllabi of the subjects of science are miles away from this scientific attitude. Today if we talk of imparting education in science, technology and vocational streams through the medium of mother tongue, it is considered nothing less than a crime. In such an adverse atmosphere, All India Council for Technical Education (AICTE) allowed education of engineering in Hindi. The government of Madhya Pradesh set the ball rolling by following this in its technical university. Both the organisations deserve our thanks. All the linguists and educationists of the world, iconic educational thinkers and education commissions of Bharat have advocated education through the medium of the mother tongue. Shiksha Sanskriti Utthan Nyas has also undertaken initiative to further this scientific notion. With this view this book was also written, first of all, in Hindi. If All India Council for Technical Education or any similar organisation finds it useful, it can be translated into other languages also.

Traditional Bharatiya thought is useful not only for Bharat, but it may be useful for the entire world. A Bharatiya delegation under the leadership of the then Prime Minister P. V. Narasimha Rao had once participated in the international convention on environment organised by United Nations Organisation on annual basis. When scholars were deliberating on environmental issues, Shri Narasimha Rao said that if the world wanted to get an effective solution to this problem, it will have to come to Bharat. He further said that in our country a child, when he wakes up on his bed, before putting his feet on the ground, he chants this *shloka*—"समुद्रवसने देवि! पर्वतस्तनमण्डले। विष्णु पत्नि नमस्तुभ्यं पादस्पर्शं क्षमस्वमे॥" This means, "Oh Mother Earth, Oh Devi, you who have the ocean as your garments, and mountains as your bosom, O consort of Lord Vishnu, salutation to you, please forgive my touch of the feet on earth, which is your holy body". His feet touch the earth under the compulsion that he has to conduct his daily activities. This is the Bharatiya vision in practice. The thoughts of Bharatiya saints and treatises are scarcely visible these days, but have not died out. The age-old practices of offering bird—seed and water to birds, offering the first baked bread to cow, not harming flora in the night, considering the *panchboot* (the five elements of nature—क्षिति, जल, पावक, गगन, समीरा or ether, water, fire, sky, air, respectively) as manifestations of diversity and to worship them, etc. are still seen in families. These are not sheer customs, but are based on logic and scientific reasoning. The tradition of Bharatiya knowledge is part and parcel of Bharatiya culture. The core or nuclear element of Bharatiya knowledge is spiritualism. In the context of spiritualism, I have to put before you two views. Once Swami Vivekananda said, 'Doing a work with selflessness is spiritualism'. The more selfless a man is, the more spiritual he is. Only Bharat is called a spiritual nation in the whole world. Some decades back, the daily routine of a common man of our country was that he would offer flour to ants, birdseeds and water to birds and provide fodder and water to animals before thinking of taking his first meal. At the time of eating, every man separated a part of his food for cow feed, while drawing water from well filled the pot for pets, and so on. In other words, while doing every work, he thought of others instead of concentrating on and being limited to, his own self. This attitude was natural and spontaneous. When a man has a habit of caring for others while doing something for himself, how can he harm or impair nature? Guided by this principle and attitude, he used to take from nature only as much as it was essential for him. This resulted in natural conservation of environment. Mahatma Gandhi said, "Nature can very well fulfil our needs, but it cannot fulfil our greeds". Contrary to this Bharatiya attitude, a western (English) philosopher and scientific thinker, Francis Bacon, advocated maximum exploitation of nature because it is the prime resource for man. This attitude is the main reason behind the problem of environment. Unless the prevailing attitude of epicurean indulgence is not disciplined, the problem of environment is impossible to solve. In the *Ishopanishad*, a view has been put forward like a formula—तेन व्यक्तेन भुंजीथा:, i.e., thou shouldst enjoy with renouncement. Only this Bharatiya attitude is capable of resolving the menace to environment.

My second view regarding environment is that, we should realise our own self—who am I? Why am I? Why I came in this world? What is the significance of my life? The practical model of this notion has, to some extent, been given in this book. The syllabi prepared by Shiksha Sanskriti Utthan Nyas for classes 1 to 12, delineate in greater detail this Bharatiya notion at the outset of every lesson. At the conclusion of every lesson, practical activities have been listed. I recommend what teachers and students have to do in their personal, familial and social life after teaching and learning of these lessons. Developing a view like this is also spiritualism. Man of today has become extrovert. We have abandoned the practice of inward thinking. We habitually comment on what our Prime Minister or American President is doing, but we have no time to think on what we did the whole day. Do we spare ten to twenty minutes at he end of the day to consider what we did on the day was improper or proper? In order to develop this habit, the contents and structure of the courses and syllabi should be spiritual. With this purpose, relevant activities should be appended to every lesson which will make teachers and students introvert and inward looking. The nature and habit of looking inwards must be developed. This signifies spiritual attitude.

Today's man faces personal, familial and societal problems, whose solution he searches in the outer world beyond his inner self. It proves futile. Solution is never available outside. It is very much available inside ourself. All the luminaries and saints of the world never cared for what the world was doing, but only thought about what they ought to do. This enabled them to successfully work towards solution to problems of the self and of the entire world. This means spiritual attitude.

But in the present times, our education and all formal systems are far removed from the fundamental thoughts of Bharat. Unless this is incorporated in their principle and practice, it is not possible for the world to solve the issue of environment.

—18 Nov, 2020

□

Eradication of Corruption and Education

Corruption is at its climax in the country. Corruption has become the goal of life. Sometime back, an opinion was floated that corruption cannot be made an issue of public agitation. But in the second stint of UPA government, corruption was rampant out of which many scandals were unravelled while the political leaders involved in them crossed all limits in faking innocence and those defending them also went beyond the limits of civility. Public protest against this was aired and led by public figures like Baba Ramdev and Anna Hazare. These great people earned unimaginable support of people. Presently, we need similar agitations. The idea sought to be popularised in society that corruption is not an issue of agitation was shattered by the common man. Movement against corruption made the common man aware of this horrid ugliness of public life. Dr. Subramanian Swamy played an important role in dragging such corrupt leaders to court and sending some of them behind the bars. Some corrupt politicians and bureaucrats did go to jail, but those, many times more in number, are still enjoying the cool comfort of power. Therefore, there is a popular demand for framing a more effective law for prevention of corruption. Perhaps, the institution of the Lok Pal may address this problem to a certain extent. If the institution of Lokayukt were not there in Uttar Pradesh and Karnataka, it would never have been possible to unseat the ruling elite and sue them in court of law.

But a pertinent question—can the willingness and inclination for corrupt practices, which is embedded in the common man's mind, be removed? I just recall an incident. I was coming to Delhi from Nagpur by Rajdhani Express Train. There were four or five co-travellers with me. A discussion began as to which political leader is most corrupt. Common opinion was that all political parties are equally involved in corruption. A gentleman put a question—what do you do if you do not get a confirmed birth when your journey is unavoidable? Running after a travel agent or TTE also does not confirm the ticket, he added. A shocking and bizarre solution was suggested by the very person who sounded most revolutionary against corruption in our earlier discussion. His suggestion was to offer ₹ 500 to the coach attendant instead of running after travel agent or TTE. He was confident that this solution never fails you. This shows the mindset of the common man in his personal life. Such an attitude of parents makes their children imbibe such unethical, dishonest and corrupt tendencies in their practical living. Sometimes, a phone call of a lender is received by a child, but the father instructs him to tell the caller that the father is not available. From this, the child learns that one should tell a lie without hesitation in order to save one's skin. Here is another anecdote to elucidate the same matter. A student visited his friend's house whose sister had recently got engaged. He asked his friend's father as to what his prospective son-in-law did. The father replied that the would-be groom was an engineer in PWD. His salary, he told, was just ₹ 12000 a month, but he had extra (underhand!) monthly income of 15 to 20 thousand rupees. It is just a matter of imagination what impact this would have made on the young student's mind and thought. Such incidents are common in our day-to-day life. People indulging in such unethical acts have no sense of wrong-doing, no pricking of conscience! This also is doubtful if the people agitating against corruption are themselves above corrupt practices in their personal life. How can corruption, which is embedded so deep, be removed? Until the root cause of the corruption, and the source of its origin in people's mind, is not identified and corrected, a permanent solution is nearly impossible. Corruption exists in the mindset. Hence, solution needs to be directed towards this problem. It is well nigh impossible to solve this problem without this.

In the Bharatiya tradition, there used to be three centres for imparting education and *sanskar*—(i) family (ii) school (iii) society. When Macaulay's policy of anglicised education system was introduced, no big damage was visible in the beginning because the other two centres of edification, family and society, continued to 'sanskarise' their children with the conventional Bharatiya doctrines, as the parents or seniors were unaffected by Macaulayism. But with the passage of time, the children trained and indoctrinated by anglicised educational system became parents. Now such people are grandfathers, grandmothers and great grandparents. Now they head the family and society too. Consequently, the primal sources of traditional *sanskar* gradually dried up. Lack of traditional Bharatiya *sanskar* in the citizen of the country created these problems which are related to ethics. The natural conclusion of the foregoing argument is that faulty education system is the root cause of such problems facing the country at large. The education of a country devoid of the inputs of *sanskar*, character, values, morality, ethics and spiritualism will naturally face the problems we are struggling with today. It is high time we correct it right now, else the situation in coming days is likely to worsen to appalling degree. If effective measures for correction are not initiated now, we should be prepared to face dangerous results in future.

The preceding discourse makes it pretty clear that—'If we have to change the country, education will have to be changed'. This is the motto of our organisation. When education of the country was inclusive of *sanskar*, morality and human values, people were rich with *sanskar* and the country was materially prosperous. There is an old folk tale of Raka and Bonka. They were husband and wife. They were travelling on foot from one village to another. The husband on the way saw a piece of gold ornament lying on the ground. Fearing that his wife may become greedy for gold, he hid it with soil. The wife was just following him. She asked him what he was doing. Those days people did not tell a lie. So, the husband narrated what he actually did. The wife replied, "You are putting dust on dust?" There is a saying in our land—other's wealth is like dust. This was not merely a proverb, but people followed its purport in practical life. There is another story from the modern times. Some college students visited a village to see their life. When they went to a farm, they saw that a bullock was rotating in circulatory way, and water was coming out from a well. The farmers were working far away. The students asked those farmers as to how they would know if the bullock stopped moving. The farmer replied that a bell is hanging on his neck and if it stops chiming, he would know that the bullock had stopped. The students shot another question, "If the bullock keeps chiming the bell in standing position, then?" The farmer innocently replied, "My bullock has not studied in a modern college". It contains an irony with far-reaching meaning. The students are not at fault. The education given to them is faulty.

A popular perception has developed in the country that more a person is educated, the more corrupt he is. In the big scandals of corruption that surfaced in the recent past, the people involved were not uneducated. Sometimes one feels that a less educated person is relatively less corrupt. A few months back, I had gone to Jamnagar in Gujarat. From there I had to go to some other place. My co-workers were not free to accompany me. So they seated me in an auto rickshaw while fixing the fare for my destination. Midway, I diverted my route and changed my destination which had a very bad road. I requested the auto driver to leave me quite before my destination because the road was in bad shape. But he insisted on taking me to the last point of my destination. After arriving there, I gave him ₹ 20, which was fixed by my co-worker. The auto driver refused to accept it and told me to give him only ₹ 10. I argued that he should take what was initially fixed. But he said that the actual distance of my travel was shorter than that of my earlier planned destination. Therefore, he added, that he would take only ten rupees which was the actual fare for this journey. He told me that he avoids ill-begotten money. Deeply impressed by his conviction, I thanked him and gave him ten rupees.

If we have to solve all the problems of the nation, and not only corruption, we need to transform education. Let us participate in the movement against corruption to begin with. But if we have to eradicate it completely, let us pledge to transform education.

—3 Nov, 2014

□

The Policy of Minority Appeasement in Education: A Vicious Design

In most of the countries of the world, there is a bitter conflict between the majority and the minority communities simply because there is blatantly unfair injustice with the minorities and they are treated as inferior, second grade citizens. In Shri Lanka, the Tamils had, initially begun their struggle for equal rights only. Similarly, in Malaysia, the condition of Hindus is alike, who are compelled to strive for equity. The Hindus of Malaysia are subjected to severe oppression, as a result they are constrained to flee from there and seek asylum in Bharat. But Bharat is a queer exception in this context, where minorities enjoy more rights and privileges than the majority community. Here the majority community is struggling for equal rights. But when they demand common civil laws, they are maligned by branding it a communal action. Those who protect and advocate minority appeasement are acclaimed as secular.

In the education sector also, the scenario is much the same. When the constitution was adopted after Independence, special rights for opening minority educational institutions were enshrined in Articles 29 & 30. Under these articles, both religious and linguistic minorities are protected. As the proviso of these articles lack articulate import, they began to be rampantly abused by misinterpreting them. The Supreme Court, the Union Government and the State Governments are shifting the responsibility of clarifying the law to one another.

It appears as if the judiciary has also come under the influence of the policy of appeasement. These two classes of minority, or others in their name, are using this law in wrong way. There are many minority institutions run by trusts which have just one trustee from the minority, besides teachers and students also have the majority community in greater number, yet the institution has the status of Minority special. Since the UPA government came to power in 2007, there is a rat race among political parties and organisations supporting them to champion this brand of minority policy. This is also intriguing that any political outfit or the court strategically eludes any comment on this. Here are some examples to show how our textbooks are loaded in favour of the minority in utter denigration of the majority's honour and criminal disrespect of historical facts:

Portions of the History Books of NCERT

- **Social Science (Part I); Medieval History (Class VIII); author Romila Thapar**

  Page-4: Akbar was eager to forge friendly relation with Rajputs. He found out a way for this in establishing marital relationship between his family and the Rajputs. He himself married many Hindu princesses. This policy of entering into political alliance consolidated his position to a great extent.

  Page-5: After demise of the seventh Guru, Aurangzeb reaped advantage from the conflict among his heirs.

- **Social Science (Part I); Modern History (Class VII); authors: Arjun Dev, Indira Arjun Dev**

  Some leaders of the *Garam Dal* of the Congress utilised religious faith and festivals to promote nationalism. This gave an opportunity to the pro-British Muslims to say that the national movement was entirely of the Hindus and, hence Muslims should not associate with it.

- **Mediveal History (Class XI); Author: Prof. Satish Chandra, page 316:** Unlike his predecessors, Aurangzeb disliked pomp and show. His personal life was very simple. He was famous as an orthodox and God-fearing Muslim. Later on he came to be called 'a living saint'.

  Page 328: This is also said that Aurangzeb was unhappy with Guru because he had converted some Muslims into Sikhs. One tradition also says that Guru had aired a voice of protest against the Governor of Kashmir who was oppressing the Hindus. But any reference of oppression of the Hindus is not available in the history of Kashmir.

  Page 330: It is doubtful that the atrocious treatment with the two sons of Guru was done by Vazir Khan under orders from Aurangzeb. It appears that Aurangzeb did not wish total annihilation of Guru, and he had written a letter to the Subedar to bring him to right path through dialogue and counselling.

  Page 337: Afzal Khan and Shivaji had resorted to deceit and fraudulence on some earlier occasions too.

  Page 341: Aurangzeb did not give any importance to friendly relation with the Marathas. In his view, Shivaji was a petty landlord.

  Page 356: Aurangzeb had a conservative outlook. He tried to act within the decorum of Islamic precepts.

  Page 328: The Battle of Haldighati was not one between the Hindus and Muslims, or the Bharatiyas and the foreigners.

- **Modern India (Class X); Author: Bipan Chandra**

  Page 20: Ranjit Singh used to dust the shoes of Muslim ascetics after walking down from his throne.

- **In the Hindi Book of NCERT, the biography of Fida Hussain is being taught.**

New Book of NCERT—Our Past—2

Out of 154 pages of this book, only 5 lines are for Chhatrapati Shivaji while 60 pages have been devoted to Mughal Dynasty.

Controversial recommendations of Sachar Committee have been included in the NCERT textbooks for class VIII.

- **Open Learning School (Delhi University); BA (Pass); History; year II; Question-2, Study Material—3 (PP 22 to 33)**

  A section of Congress was responsible for pushing the Muslims towards communalism. It is true that Congress was a secular organisation but large number of its members comprised of those who were orthodox and were influenced by the feelings of Hindusim. The basis of Ghandhiji's secularism was not scientific. His proposition of Swaraj on the principles of Ramrajya could not enthuse the Muslims. The politically backward Muslims were induced to separatism by Hindu religious feelings.

  Hindu Communal forces had a considerable role in intensifying communal feelings among the Muslims.

- After Hindu Mahasabha was founded, it began massive propaganda against Muslims.
- One more Hindu communal organisation took birth. This organisation was Rashtriya Swayamsevak Sangh. As an organisation, it proved more effective in spreading communalism.
- Jawahar Lal Nehru was the Prime Minister, but Patel run the home ministry at his own will. He did not use his powers to quell communal riots, but to aggravate them, to promote Rashtriya Swayamsevak Sangh and to prove that Muslims were habitual riot-mongers.

*Other Measures of the Union Government For Minority Appeasement

- Students of other communities get education loan at the interest rate of 12-14 per cent, while those of the minority community get it at the rate of 3 per cent.
- The logo of Kendriya Vidyalaya Sangathan had the image of the sun and a lotus, which was changed to a cross and half-moon with a star.
- Madarsas, which are not a component of any formal education system, have been given equal status with the constituents of Kendriya Vidyalaya Sangathan.
- In 2005, 50 per cent reservation was introduced for Muslim students in Aligarh Muslim University, which is against the principles of the Constitution.
- Aligarh Muslim University has been granted ₹ 2000 crore to open its regional centres at Bhopal, Pune, Kishanganj, Murshidabad and Mallapuram. The respective states have been asked to provide 500 acres of land without charging its cost.
- The UPA government constituted Minority Education Commission in 2004.
- On 20th January, 2009, the Vice President of Bharat, speaking at the annual convention of National Minorities Commission, suggested that a separate set of laws should be enacted for Minority communities. He further suggested that Law against Atrocities on Scheduled Caste and Scheduled Tribes made in 1989 should also be made for Minorities.

* Measures of State Governments for Minority Appeasement

- In Rajasthan, pre-secondary scholarship to minority students are given on mere affidavit of the parents.
- Andhra Pradesh government has earmarked a reservation of 4 per cent in educational institutions.

In the schools run by social welfare department, 12 per cent reservation has been created for converted students, depriving the social sections for whom these schools run.

- Tamil Nadu government allotted 7 per cent seats to minorities by curtailing the share of other backward classes.
- West Bengal government has proposed to earmark 30 per cent of the budget allocation of every department for minorities. It also proposed to allot all vacant government land to minorities.
- Aliha University was established by the Government of West Bengal in 17th December, 2007.
- On 12th March, 2008, the Finance Minister of West Bengal, Asim Dasgupta, while presenting Budget Estimates for 2008-09, proposed to establish 200 madarsas of higher secondary level. He further opined that 300 centres of secondary education should be set up in those areas in which minorities were in majority.
- The government of Bihar has announced full free student-ship to minority students of classes 10 and 12 in the four districts of Purnea, Araria, Katihar and Kishanganj.
- In Bihar again a cash prize of ₹ 10,000 is being offered to minority students passing 10th examination.
- On the recommendation of Pololi Committee of Kerela, formed for implementation of the recommendation of Sachar Committee, Muslim girl student doing graduate and post graduate courses were given scholarship of ₹ 5000. Girl students of vocational courses will receive a scholarship of ₹ 4000. Initially, the number of this scholarship has been limited to 5000, which will increase to 15000 the next year.
- Girl students of Muslim Community of Kerala residing

in hostel for preparation of competitive examinations are being awarded a scholarship of ₹ 10,000 while those for pursuing regular courses are awarded a scholarship of ₹ 1000.

—28 June, 2009

□

Educational Transformation: Future Road Map

Shiksha Bachao Andolan Samiti was constituted on 2nd July, 2004. In a short period of four years, it earned nationwide recognition as a conscious and effective organisation. Teachers, students, parents and educationists expect this organisation to emerge as a potent medium for educational transformation in the country in the following years.

In its initial phase, Shiksha Bachao Andolan raised protest against distortion in textbooks and study material, struggled in various ways for their rectification, and achieved commendable success. It spearheaded countrywide agitation against objectionable portion and distorted information in the history books of NCERT leading to victory in judicial contests. Likewise, it struggled for the removal of objectionable untruth about Hindu Gods and Goddesses, and compelled the government to withdraw them. The pressure of their protest was so massive that the Human Resource Development Minister had to announce this withdrawal in the Parliament within eight days. Public awareness programmes and agitations were organised in the whole country against the Central Government's vicious attempt to introduce sex education in a distorted form. Consequently, eleven states refused to introduce it in their respective states. The central government was also compelled to review its decision. Objection was formally filed against the textbooks of National Open School which called the revolutionaries as extremists.

The textbooks of Odisha branded Rashtriya Swayamsevak Sangh, Vishva Hindu Parishad, Bajrang Dal, Bharatiya Janata Party as communal organisations. We struggled against this through vehement protest which compelled the government to act as we desired.

Shiksha Bacho Andolen has always endeavoured through democratic mode to bring about positive transformation in the education sector. Creation of public awareness about issues in education is an accepted mode in democratic system, which we always adopted. On many subjects, we took recourse to judicial avenue in which we have received positive results from lower courts to the Supreme Court. We also made the most of democratic tools by getting suitable questions raised on our behest in the state legislative assemblies and the Parliament.

Our aim, however, is not only to stage *dharna*, taking out processions, organising demonstrations and slogan shouting to attract attention, but we do resort to such democratic methods of protest to create public awareness on relevant educational issues and to ensure their suitable resolution. At times, situation compels us to take recourse to these. When the books of National Open School termed the revolutionaries of the country as terrorists, we called upon the concerned officials to register our protest. The officers acted positively, but we never cared to publicise it as our achievement. Against history book of the correspondence course of Delhi University, we filed a representation and gave them two months' time to redress our grievance. The university administration promptly acted and made required rectification. Hence, we did not do any agitation. But sometimes our experience was exactly contrary to this. In the history book of Delhi University, Hindu gods and goddesses were denigrated and insulted. In the books of social science, women were insulted through wrong examples from the Vedas. On the twin issues, we had to resort to vehement agitation. Despite direction of the Supreme Court, the Vice

Chancellor of the university has not yet announced removal of these distortions of facts.

Our aim is not to get publicity or to do agitation with this purpose. We are endeavouring to create greater share and participation of society in the education sector, and with this end in mind, we are constantly working to make society aware of its role. So far, about 700 seminars have been organised across the country, in which more than 1.5 lakh people participated. On the issue of sex education, the Petition Committee of the Rajya Sabha received 41,000 representations and letters. Representations like these are always signed by a group of people. As such, many more people than 41,000 participated in this process. So far, 45 booklets have been published, which have been sent to 6000 people. In different parts of the country, lakhs of leaflets and pamphlets in different languages have been published. Signature campaigns were carried out on different issues. On the issue of sex education about 4,15,000 signatures were obtained, in which Jain society had a commendable contribution. In a conference organised on this subject itself, 26 institutions came together on one platform. In an NCERT book, it was written—'Jats were robbers', against which the entire Jat society of Haryana agitated. This yielded positive result too. An important person of Jain society filed a suit in the District Court of Alwar against an objectionable comment against Lord Mahavir in a textbook of NCERT. The court ruled in our favour. Likewise, against an objectionable comment against Arya Samaj and Swami Dayananda Saraswati, their followers filed a suit in the High Court of Chandigarh, which yielded positive result. Through the efforts of Shiksha Bachao Andolan, many educational issues have reverberated in the parliament and state assemblies.

We wish to mould education as per its national concept to enable it to serve society and nation in an effective way. People of the country also want this. That is the reason, more than 30 educational, social, spiritual and religious organisations and different political leadership have supported our campaign.

Owing to contortions and distortions pervading in the textbooks at state and central levels, everyone felt a need for a movement to rectify these, and all agree that this will have to be continued in the times to come. It can, of course, be said that our campaign is, in a way, a sheer reaction. But its creative aspect is that this campaign opened exhaustive debate and dialogue on education leading to wide awareness of the masses.

A thoughtful climate is gradually developing in the country in which it is being earnestly felt that society should discuss the shape and model of education, and it should also determine the benchmark of this model. This work should have begun immediately after Independence, but unfortunately it didn't. The successive governments constituted Kothari Commission, Mudaliar Commission, Radhakrishnan Commission and announced Education Policy in 1986, but the positive recommendations of all these commissions could not be implemented for want of political will.

Shiksha Sanskriti Utthan Nyas has been formed to bring about radical change in the education sector, and to offer the society a new alternative of education. In view of this objective these two efforts and action are required:

- Countrywide mass awareness about issues involving education.
- To subsume all stakeholders like students, teachers, educationists, officers of educational administration and directors of educational institutions etc. into this process of transformation to forge out a new alternative of education.

Campaign for educational transformation should be, both, decentralised and nationwide. Different institutions, universities, social organisations etc. should work together to set up a new model of educational system, to frame new policy and to determine new standard and alternative of education. With this purpose, organising seminars, dialogues, conferences, conventions etc. and preparing relevant books and literatures will be in our priority. Books and literatures prepared through such brainstorming exercise should be accepted by all private and government schools, colleges and universities and also the governments at places—we have to work in this direction. In all such endeavours, it is highly necessary that co-operation of educationists of the country, organisations active in education sectors, social-spiritual-religious outfits working in line of Bharatiya thought and conviction, businessmen and political leaders desiring improvement in education etc. is ensured. Education will have to be elevated to the first from the last in concern as it presently is.

Through all these efforts, all the distortions and fallacies permeating the educational material will be removed. Country's education will have to be made compatible with Bharatiya culture and ethos by defining the traditional trove of Bharatiya knowledge and wisdom in the modern context and made free from western influence. While preparing an alternative of education, Bharatiya languages need to be restored their lost status. The vision of Dr. A.P.J. Abdul Kalam about a developed Bharat in 2020 and to establish Bharat as a global Guru by reconstructing its dilapidated aspects are possible only through education bringing about material and spiritual prosperity.

—31 Dec, 2008

□

Proposed New Education Policy and Bharatiya Vision

Before this, education policy has been framed twice in Independent Bharat—first, in 1968 and second, in 1986. In addition to this, the central government constituted a number of commissions and committees like Radhakrishnan Commission in 1948, Mudaliar Commission in 1952, Kothari Commission in 1964, Ram Murti Committee and Yashpal Committee, besides subject/issue specific committees for educational reform. These commissions and committees made good recommendations and suggestions, but they were never implemented for lack of political will or because they did not suit the ruling elite.

After 29 years since 1986, Education Policy was again reviewed and the process of formulating a new policy was initiated. In our view, such a review should be done at the end of every ten years of its previous proposal because society and country are subject to rapid changes unfolding fast which require re-defining the education policy in the topical contexts obtaining relevance. Nonetheless, the Human Resources Development Department, the Government of Bharat, has taken up the work of bringing a new education policy. This is a welcome step. The effort of the central government to elicit opinion from the stakeholders at the base of the pyramid, down to the villages, for the proposed education policy, is highly commendable. The government had invited suggestions through its website, which yielded more than 29,000 suggestions. However, this is also experienced that barring a few state governments, the efforts in this context at the ground level is much deficient than what was required.

The Ministry of Human Resource Development has put up 13 points for school level education and 20 points for higher education on which suggestions are to be given for consideration in the proposed New Education Policy. Primary education is of greater importance than the higher education, in our humble opinion. As such, it would have been more proper if the number of issues put up for suggestions for the two levels of education ought to have been at least similar in number. In my opinion, there should have been three levels or areas for inviting suggestions. The first should be common issues relevant to education. The second should be school education. The third should be higher education. The division of levels in this manner would have been more appropriate. An observation of the issues published for suggestions hardly include those related to the aims and objectives of education. Education of Independent Bharat still lacks direction. Its main reason is the utter lack of clarity about its aims and objectives.

The nature and structure of education to become appropriate, it is necessary, in our view, that New Education Policy should include in it the following elements:

Aims and Objectives of Education

Persons of character and having holistically developed personality have a special role in the development of the country. Making such persons should be prime objective of education. In the concept of *Panchakosh* enshrined in the *Taittiriya Upanishad*, it is enumerated in an excellent way. In the opinion of Swami Vivekananda, education is means of realisation of inherent potentiality of man and his inherent potentialities are the means of country's development. Education should be such,

- that could fulfil the needs of society and nation.

- that which helps in solving the national and international challenges.
- that which is in agreement with the nation's culture, ethos and progression.
- that which enriches man's knowledge, makes his work sublime, creates his human identity and sensitises him for social co-existence.
- that which promotes national unity and integrity.

Basic Concept

Education should be autonomous at all levels. It should use mother tongue as medium of instruction. It should be value based. It should be a means of service. Besides these, education should have in it the following elements:

- It should have a comprehensive and integrative attitude.
- It should have a balanced harmony of principle and practice.
- It should integrate modern knowledge with the traditional knowledge of ancient Bharat.
- It should have a fair harmony of materialism and spiritualism.
- It should reinforce the traditional Bharatiya notion of family.
- It should align with the fundamental rights enshrined in the constitution.
- Educational planning should be in consonance with national planning.

Quality in Education

- Every child is entitled to quality education in the context of 'fundamental right to quality life'. Hence, in order to ensure common standard of quality in educational institutions, with emphasis on social participation, a suitable framework should be developed under a special programme. Under this framework, proper attention should be paid to quality of required material infrastructure simultaneous with 'real' quality of education. Special plans should be made for rural areas.

- Educational institutions at district level should be made responsible for other institutions in their area.
- Government schools and privately managed schools should not be considered as rivals of each other. Instead, academic relation between them should be strengthened for enrichment of quality in education. Besides conducting co-curricular activities at common platform, their resourses should be mutually utilised by one another and, thereby, promote academic exchange programmes.
- For evaluation and accreditation of institutions of higher learning, transparent arrangement like NAAC (National Assessment and Accreditation Council) should be expanded upto regional level. With this purpose, units of NAAC may be set up at regional level. Alternatively, a reputed central or state university of the region may be entrusted this work. Private or foreign institutions should never be a choice for this.
- For strengthening state universities, a proper arrangement should be made to meet the requirement of their resources. To monitor the usage of such aids, a vigilance unit may be set up. Institutions of higher learning like IIT, IIM, Medical College etc. should be opened in rural areas.

Curriculum/Courses of Study

- In basic lessons of all subjects at all levels, Bharat's contribution to the world in the tradition of knowledge in the areas of history, culture, science, mathematics (especially Vedic mathematics) etc. should be compulsorily included. A gist of all Bharatiya religious sects should be added to the curriculum.

- Vicious propaganda in the contents of lessons at different levels, regarding our culture, traditions, religious sects, religion and iconic saints-cum-thinkers should be removed forthwith. Stress should be laid on presenting history strictly based on right context with a non-partisan attitude.
- At all levels of formal education, courses should be relevant to the regional as well as national needs. Due emphasis should be given on making courses pragmatic and useful for life.
- It needs to be reviewed and assessed how Bharat is being represented in the course materials of foreign countries, and suitable steps should be taken to rectify the discrepancies, if any.
- Information and communication system should be made an essential part of courses at all levels.

Language Policy

- In every state, a university of its language should be established in which teaching of management, engineering and medicine should be carried out in the medium of that language itself.
- In the International Hindi University of Wardha, all vocational and professional courses should be gradually begun to be taught in Hindi.
- Legal and disciplinary action should be taken against schools which prohibit speaking in mother tongue on their campus.
- A suitable plan should be made for popularising Hindi and Sanskrit in foreign countries. The foreign institutions which are working on Bharatiya languages should be encouraged through academic collaboration.
- Three language formula should be reviewed and a new language policy should be formulated. Compulsory

status of English language should be removed from all levels of formal education.

- IIT, IIIT, NIT and IIM should also give the option of study in Hindi medium.
- In all competitive examinations and recruitment tests, option of Bharatiya language must be given.
- A policy for ensuring respectable position of Sanskrit in academics should be made.
- Medium of instruction in all the languages of the 8th Schedule should be available in Central schools.
- Schools should not give option of foreign language. Those willing to learn foreign language may be allowed to pursue Certificate or Diploma courses in the concerned language.
- The medium of exchange of thoughts and ideas in education sector should be Bharatiya languages. A suitable policy should be framed in this regard.

Financial Aspect

- A legal system should be in place to regulate fee structure in private schools and universities.
- All elected peoples' representatives—from municipal councillors to members of parliament—should be made to spend, at least 20 per cent of the Local Area Development fund granted to them on education.
- A minimum of 6 per cent of Gross Domestic Product (GDP) should be spent on education.
- In government and government-aided institutions of higher learning, the fees should be proportionate to student's financial status.

Teacher's Education and Development

- There should be mutual inter-relation between the teacher-education curriculum for pre-service and in-service teachers.

- While putting on hold the present teacher-education courses (B.Ed. and M.Ed.) of two year duration, a committee should be constituted to frame new courses which should include basic subjects, besides emphasising our educational development in the past. Teacher education should be based on national ethos.
- All schools should be compulsorily attached to a teacher education institution on a permanent basis.
- New courses for pre-service and in-service teachers' education should be introduced for teachers of teacher education colleges.
- For professional development of teachers, a policy should be made for their further education which should include a provision of sabbatical leave with full pay.
- There should be a provision of promotion of teachers from primary to secondary/higher secondary on even consideration of their merit, efficiency and proficiency.
- Appointment of part-time teachers should be completely discontinued and a concrete policy of filling up all vacancies of teachers at all levels on permanent basis should be framed.
- The quality of entrance tests should be reviewed and flaws, if any, should be removed.

Student Support

- Counselling Centres should be set up in all institutions where students should be counselled about their future life, further education and professions or vocations available to them. Student Counselling centres should be augmented with modern techniques. A network of such centres should be set up.
- A suitable support system for students of semi-urban and rural areas should be created.
- Hostels should be made available as per requirement.

- Good quality medical aid should be ensured in all educational institutions.

Basic Subjects

- Teaching of yoga as well as health and hygiene should be arranged while programmes should be made for keeping the students healthy.
- Experience of social service should be included in curriculum at all levels. Every educational institution should adopt one village or dwelling, and universities at least ten, for service.
- In the curriculum at school level beginning from class V onwards, lessons on entrepreneurship, skill development, vocational Counselling, citizen's duty and inculcation of patriotism should be included.
- The curriculum should also include basic subjects like environment, values, life-skills, physical exercise, sports and games, fine arts etc.
- In order to develop a taste and bent for self-study, there should be library in every school with a time schedule for students to use it compulsorily.
- Public library should be set up at Cluster Resource Centres and it should be linked to the school in that area.

Autonomy

- On the pattern of Judiciary and Election Commission, an autonomous 'National Education Council' should be constituted which should have its units at state and district levels.
- For autonomy in education to be sustainable and acceptable, adequate transparency and accountability should be ensured in the system.
- Quality Administration with Human Touch
- Academic administration ought to have in it human touch in required measure.

- Bharatiya Education Service should be organised with special eligibility criteria. All the posts of academic administration should be filled from this cadre.
- Any proposal to open a new educational institution should be based on, and guided by, Human Resource Survey.
- Educational administration should be reformed with incorporation of transparency, accountability and collective decision-making. To achieve this end, unwanted complication should be removed from administration.

Research Work

- Research/investigation should be linked to nation's needs. To inculcate a love for research in students at school level itself, suitable input should be incorporated in the syllabus.
- There should be adequate freedom in doing research work and there should not be any time bar. Degree should be awarded by recognising scholarly research done outside a university too.
- Research and publication should be in Bharatiya language to maximum extent. If a thesis or article is in English, it should be compulsorily translated into any one of Bharatiya languages. Strict norms should be made to ensure this.
- Policy should be made for interaction between university and industry in the context of research work.
- Artisans practising traditional arts and handicrafts should also be awarded certificates and their innovative work should be rewarded.
- It should be ensured that research work is practically utilised. System should be streamlined to carry the conclusion of research to their beneficiaries.

- Rules should be made to publish conclusions of research in a national journal first, and afterwards it may be published in the international ones.

Evaluation System

- There should be a sensible cohesion of observation, activity and formal examination at all levels.
- The policy of not detaining unsuccessful students from classes I to VIII should be reviewed and reconsidered.
- Semester system in higher education should be reviewed and instead of implementing it at once, it should be enforced gradually. As an experiment, it may first be implemented at post-graduate level, preceded by sufficient preparation.
- CBCS and Grade Point system should not be made compulsory in higher education. Sufficient preparation should be made for this and it should be implemented in gradual process.

Admission Process

- Every student should get equal opportunity for education.
- The process of admission should be simple.
- Admission through donation and capitation fee should be banned under law.
- The concept of school in the neighbourhood should be brought into practice.

Miscellaneous Points

- Pre-primary education should be included in 'Right to Free and Compulsory Education'.
- 'Right to Free and Compulsory Education Act-2009' must be reviewed and necessary amendment should be introduced in it.
- A proper system of direct and face-to-face teaching

should be introduced in Open Schooling System. A provision to give education in all the languages of the 8th Schedule of the Constitution should be made.

- Adult education programme should, besides developing literacy, develop a proficiency of reading and writing.
- The curriculum for learners' of Scheduled Caste and Scheduled Tribe communities and those living in difficult hilly terrains should be compatible to their specific needs and in their own language. If study material is not available in their language, it may be in the state's official language, but their own language should be used for communication in the teaching-learning process.
- For differently-abled and socially-deprived section of children a policy specific to their needs should be evolved.
- For developing a *sanskar*-wise rich atmosphere in school, and developing a sense of family on the campus, a definite policy, programme and planning need to be evolved. With this end in mind, the following action may be considered:
  - Right from primary education to higher education, morning assembly and concerned activities like prayer, yoga etc. should be made compulsory.
  - Programmes to celebrate Guru Purnima, Raksha Bandhan etc. should be institutionalised.
  - On the walls inside the school inspiring quotes, sketches of iconic persons and sketches related to folk tales for children should be inscribed.
  - Programme to welcome freshers should be organised.
  - In technical stream of education, there should be arrangement for practical, hands-on work experience.

- The study material of distance and online learning modes should be in Bharatiya languages.

Education is a potent means of social change. As is the education, so will the country be. The root cause of most of the problems of the country at present is faulty education. Hence we say, if we have to change the country, we must change education. The first prerequisite of this is that Bharatiya vision should guide policy making. Secondly, framing a policy alone will not serve the purpose but its implementation on ground is the real challenge. As such, any announcement of a policy should be accompanied by a blueprint to translate it into reality, with committees and sub-committees to monitor this process. The committees and sub-committees should ensure the implementation of policy in the given time-frame.

Education is not a subject of only government, but it concerns the entire society, especially the people directly related to education sector should have an important role in it. For implementation of a policy, it is necessary to create a suitable mindset of the society and to obtain their co-operation. In the same way, as suggestions have been elicited from society upto villages for framing the policy, their participation is also required in its implementation. The committee overseeing the implementation should also think on this. We hope that the government must have considered taking steps in this very direction.

—18 Feb, 2017

□

State of Education: Changes and Directions

शिक्षा पा कर भिक्षा माँगे, युवजन खाएँ ठोकर आज।
आज़ादी का स्वप्न दिखाकर, पाखंडी करते हैं राज॥
भ्रष्ट व्यवस्था ने भी, डाला अब यहाँ डेरा है।
चलो जलाएँ दीप वहाँ, जहाँ अभी भी अँधेरा है॥

[Educated yough stumble, are compelled to beg,
Imposters cheat with false notion of liberty, and rule,
Corrupt system is firmly entrenched all around,
Let's light a lamp where darkness still prevails.]

We are endeavouring to level the hiatus between the objectives of education and its present condition in which we all teach. When the blackboard is clean, it is easy to write something new on it. But when wrong matter is written on the blackboard, it needs to be erased before something right may be written on it. In our education system also, such contortions and distortions have been inserted, not by aliens and foreigners, but by some people of our own country following a certain school of thought. Such things are prevailing without any interruption even after 73 years of Independence. The British taught us that the Aryans came from some foreign land and they chased away the Dravidas. They taught us so to drive home the logic that since we, the Aryans, are ourselves foreigners, what justification is there in calling them foreigners and invaders? It is unfortunate that this logic is being perpetuated till now in our teaching. The revolutionary nationalists like Lal, Bal and Pal etc. are termed extremists in NCERT books.

Shiksha Bacho Andolan Samiti began an agitation against this. Consequently, lakhs of students were saved from reading this distorted information. From NCERT books of history, some 75 pieces of such misinformation were removed. All these expunged portions denigrated and maligned our culture, religion and iconic persons. In the syllabus of BA (Hons), second year, distorted information about characters of the *Ramayana* is being served to students. This is being done under national and international conspiracy. Our religion, culture and traditions are noble. A lobby of the west and a group following a certain stream of thinking envy our superiority. If characters of the *Ramayana* are presented in a bad light, how can our children respect them? If our students today are asked as to who was the first and the last Mughal King or British viceroy, they can give correct answer. But if they are aksed to name the four Vedas, or if Jain students are asked to name the 24 Jaina Tirthankars, they will draw a blank. This is a planned conspiracy to kill Bharatiya self-respect. When a set of misinformation that our countrymen lacked *sanskar* and education, our gods and deities were also like this, is planted in the minds of our children, how can they take pride in their country? If we talk of Vedic mathematics in our country, it is defamed as communalism. But when a foreign scholar, impressed by Vedic mathematics, delivered a lecture on the subject, it came to be noticed in the country. People of Bharat have a false idea that things of the west are superior to those of ours. Dr. A.P.J. Abdul Kalam wrote in his book that a calendar hung on the wall of his house. It was printed in Germany. Anyone who saw this praised Germany because the photograph on the calendar was impressive. Then Dr. Kalam asked them to read what was printed in small letters below the photograph. After reading that they would exclaim if the photograph was really taken by a Bharatiya! There is a general mentality in our country to consider people speaking English as scholars and those speaking in Bharatiya language as rustics. Addressing one's parents as *mata* and *pita* is considered old-fashioned and calling them Mummy and Papa shows modernity. If they are called Mom and Dad, it is ultra-modern. The whole world is accepting Vedic mathematics today. If children are taught mathematics thorough Vedic method, they will enjoy the subject and will comfortably solve the questions of mathematics.

A more serious work is being done on this subject in countries like Germany, England etc. Some scholars of our country ask, "Why it is named Vedic Mathematics?" In our country, every dialogue begins with controversy. Let us keep ourselves engaged in fighting while a person from America has filed a petition for patent of one stream of Vedic Mathematics. Therefore I repeat, wrong things are written on the blackboard and only erasing them will not solve our purpose. We will have to do concrete work by writing right things afresh on the blackboard. Just by talking of Bharatiya education, education will not be Bharatised. Our fundamental principles of education, which are deeply rooted in ancient wisdom, are eternal truth having perennial relevance. But they need to be modified and moulded into a new system or structure in the context of modern needs of modern times. In a way, a sensible synthesis of the antiquity and the contemporary needs to be contrived. Such a synthesis in the context of all subjects of study will generate a novel system of Bharatiya education with a distinct modern outlook. This will be acceptable to the whole world. Working in this direction, the Shiksha Sanskriti Utthan Nyas, in collaboration with different institutions , has organised six symposia. Out of these, one was organised in Banaras Hindu University in an adverse situation, but its impact was so positive that in its valedictory session, a professor, conveying a vote of thanks, requested us to organise such a symposium of four days' duration instead of one day's.

the Dean of the Faculty proposed to include it in the syllabus. Shiksha Sanskriti Utthan Nyas plans to set up research centre dedicated to Vedic Mathematics which will develop its syllabus from standards 1 to 12 and for higher education. The research centre will also work on 'Vedic Mathematics for Computer'. In the next step it is planned to include Vedic Mathematics in the curricula at post-school level. Only if we work like this, it will be accepted in the country as well as the whole world. A parallel effort is required to introduce it in government schooling system. The following four tangible benefits can be reaped from the books of a course in Vedic Mathematics:

- Formation of *sanskar* in students.
- Greater discipline in students.
- A positive improvement in students' examination result.
- Positive impact on teacher who teaches the subject.

Without such concrete work on ground, a call for a Bharatiya kind of education is imperfect. So, we need to study all related issues deeply and seriously. Teacher, or *acharya*, is the key to transformation in education. All of us are teachers. But in the modern scenario, the work of giving education has come to be treated as business. But actually it is a mission, not a business. Giving education is the best work. It has the potential to transform man. We should have a sense of glory on this account. We will have to accomplish this work with utmost devotion. Teachers working with due assiduity have transformed the world. A school principal once told me that students do not come to school. In my reply, I put a poser—"Why will they come?" The fact is that for the last 150 years, students are subject to the same stereotyped system in which they listen to 40-minute lecture period-wise, and return home. Novelty needs to be introduced in the teaching method. In the ancient Bharat, we had 32 methods of teaching. Teaching was executed also through experiments. In Gujarat, Vidya Bharati is doing an experiment in some schools in which students come to school without any reading or writing material with them, and go back in the same way. In these schools, small children are taught history through portraits. Numerical tables are chanted to the accompaniment of tabla and harmonium. Students enjoy learning through novel experiments. Teaching through these methods gives immeasurable pleasure to teachers also. Teachers should change their approach to, and attitude towards, teaching. They should give equal attention to all students. If our mind is not fully concentrated and it is roaming outside, teaching will be unproductive and ineffective. Teacher is a psychologist in practice. He has to gauge the students' phychology and mental state on each day. A leader or *acharya* has to play dual role of mother and father. Once a student came to see Malaviyaji. He expressed his inability to pay examination fee. His teachers had the opinion that he came of a well-to-do family, and so he was misleading them. He had ample money but he was in the habit of frittering it away on wrong things. Malaviyaji finally ruled, "This student is studying in our institution for some years. Even then he has such habits. Are we also not somehow responsible for this? He should be permitted to take examination". It is necessary to develop such an attitude towards students. Acharya Vinoba Bhave said, the one who teaches through his conduct is the real *acharya*. Once Prof. Yashwant Rao Kelkar gave some money to a student. After some time, he began his business and came to him to return the money. Prof. Kelkar refused to take the money and advised him to help needy students with that amount. There is no metal which does not melt. It only needs as much heat as it requires to melt. The solutions of problems facing the country are possible only through education. Students should be taught and inspired to stop misuse of water and electricity. Students can be given practical education through small acts and affairs. It is also required to educate children about developing social and national attitude in their general thought. A 40-minute lecture will never suffice. Some experiments in the direction of social change need to be taken up. The chanting of *Omkar* three times by students in the beginning of every period may go a long way in disciplining them and improving their concentration.

Drastic change in education is a big issue. Do all of us have a Bharatiya attitude about ourselves? We need to deeply contemplate in this direction: Any change will begin with that in ourselves. In our common chat, we use English words. The struggle of language is prolonged. The struggle needs to be begun with ourselves. We should mark our signature in Hindi. Nowadays, the word 'India' is common. Proper name cannot be translated in any language. We may have some compulsion for writing or speaking in English. But in English also, we should name Bharat as our country. Change begins from small instances.

Transformation of education is a divine work. If country is to be re-developed and it has to regain its lost seat of the mentor of the world, education must be transformed. Macaulay knew that it was difficult to rule Bharat without changing education. Therefore, he changed the pattern of education first and also changed the medium of education. In place of Sanskrit schools, English schools were opened. In a letter to his father, he wrote that he was immensely happy to change the pattern of Bharat's education, but he will consider it his real success when the pattern of education introduced by him sustained when they would have left Bharat. Those educated in his system would remain Bharatiya in looks but in thought, behaviour, manners and overall demeanour, they will be thoroughly non-Bharatiya. Hence, change in education is the first and foremost requirement. As teachers, this becomes our greater responsibility. We pray that you should seriously think on the ways and means of positive change in education.

—5 Feb, 2015

□

Vocational Education in the Report of Rashtriya Gyan Ayog

The National Knowledge Commission (NKC) presented its report on Vocational Education in two distinct parts. One was on Vocational Education, while the other was on Professional Education. At school level, it made suggestions regarding Vocational Education and in the context of Professional Education, it gave suggestions, more for medical, legal and management streams, and very little for engineering and pharmacy streams.

Vocational Education

The recommendation is that vocational education should be entirely in the domain of Ministry of Human Resource Development, because presently the institutions like ITIs are under Ministry of Labour and Employment. In fact, all the courses of education should be under one ministry, and the name of the ministry should be Education Ministry instead of MHRD. The Knowledge Commission emphasised the need of setting up National Council for Vocational Training and Employment for Development of Vocational Education. For streamlining training, an autonomous Regulatory Agency was also recommended.

The Commission made a very important recommendation that there should be a thorough study of manpower available in the country and the financial outlay in 11th Five Year

Plan should be carefully and sensibly based on this. About expenditure, they recommended that 10 to 15 per cent of the expenditure should be on vocational education. Other recommendations of the Commission include enhancement of tuition fee, collaboration of trade and industry, needs of the market etc. They further recommended that vocational education should be accorded equal importance with secondary education. It also recommended that for Vocational Education, the words Skill Development should be used.

Legal Education

NKC has considered legal education an important component of Professional Education. They held the Bar Council of India (BCI) responsible for the present plight of legal education. The BCI, they opine, has neither any specialisation in, nor any powers to, address international challenges. Hence, they favoured setting up a new regulatory authority. They also recommended setting up an autonomous agency for evaluation, accreditation and ranking of legal institutions. For preparing courses and syllabi of legal studies, the NKC recommended establishment of a National Law School. It also suggested that a model syllabus should be framed with a view to orient legal studies towards society and at the same time to sensitise students for social justice. For this, they recommended taking feedback from students. They recommended improvement in examination system by orienting it to the needs of current times as well as modern principles. They advocated establishing Legal Study and Research Centre. As an important suggestion, they favoured collaboration of Bharatiya institutions with foreign ones and awarding joint or dual degrees.

Medical Education

NKC has made some important recommendations for improvement in medical education. Even after 73 years of Independence, medical facility has not evenly reached villages. Admitting this deficiency, they recommended launching rural medical programme and also providing training to rural medical practitioners in the medical colleges. All private medical colleges should give details of their fees in the brochure, they suggested. They also suggested organising a general entrance test at national level for seats in private medical colleges. The government should strike a regional balance in availability and quality of medical colleges. The government should establish at least one medical institution of excellence in every state, they added.

Now the question arises as to how an Independent and standardised entrance examination can be conducted at the national level in a huge country like Bharat? Its feasibility needs to be examined. They also recommended that every medical professional should undergo a re-certification process four years after obtaining the basic degree. It needs to be examined if this proposal is practically acceptable.

One significant recommendation they made is that 20 per cent seats for Post Graduate courses should be reserved for medical professionals having rendered their services in rural areas for three years after completing graduate course. A recommendation of NKC worth consideration is that the Medical, Dental and Pharmacy Councils should supervise and regulate only granting licence to people willing to enter their profession whereas supervision and regulatory responsibility of medical education should be given to a permanent committee constituted specifically for this purpose, which will function under Independent Regulatory Authority for Higher Education (IRAHE).

Management Education

Before the year 2000, there were only 700 management colleges which have now proliferated to 1,700. Most of these institutions are compromising with quality and standards of academics. The NKC admitted that a commercial attitude and intention of exploitation have unfortunately crept in these institutes. For regulating this stream of education as well, a permanent committee of autonomous nature, and within it a Management Education Authority, should be constituted. They recommended that this authority should also offer scholarship to socially deprived students.

To ensure availability of qualified teachers in management colleges also, the NKC has stressed the formation of an autonomous authority. They also recommended that barring the management departments in the universities, all management institutes should be accorded autonomous status. In order to expand the geographical area and increasing its priority level among prospective learners of management sciences, facility of online study and teaching, adjusting the contents of management courses to regional requirements, addition of courses in health management as well as co-operative management should be ensured, they recommended.

Other Professional Streams

NKC opined that the model of engineering education had become outdated and, therefore, less useful. They emphasised remodeling engineering courses and curriculum with futuristic vision. They also recommended increasing the role of paramedical personnel. For this, they suggested including it as a subject at higher secondary level, besides making suitable arrangement for practical training of the passout and setting up Paramedical Council as apex regulatory authority. They recommended a massive increase in seats for pharmacy education.

Conclusion

The Commission admitted the failure of the system of vocational and professional education. It recommended constitution of various types of regulatory bodies while curtailing the powers and functions of old bodies like AICTE, Bar Council of India (BCI), Medical Council of India (MCI) etc. Besides, they favoured augmentation of quality in education and promotion of research. In many cases, they have suggested to address the needs of the market. The question naturally arises, is vocational or professional education meant for market alone? They also referred to participation or collaboration of foreign universities, but to make it practically possible, the country, as of now, lacks suitable legal provisions. How can this take effect in reality unless law of the land permits this? The pragmatic value of many such recommendations are doubtful and deserve to be questioned. The report of the Commission does not contain detailed description of many of its recommendations.

Our Suggestions

The National Knowledge Commission, in fact, made a superficial collection of matters from sundry sources here and there and based its recommendations on it. It was highly imperative that it should have done serious thinking on vocational education, quality aspect of institutions, commercialisation of education, present state of educational system, geographical imbalance in location of institutions etc., and should have put forward concrete plan for their correction and improvement.

As per data for the year 2006, out of 1346 engineering colleges in the country, as many as 922 were situated in the states of Kerala, Karnataka, Tamil Nadu, Andhra Pradesh and Maharashtra. In the colleges of these states located at small centres, very few students, compared to available seats, are seeking admission. The result is that these colleges award degree to students with lesser competence than what is required, simply in order to survive in the market. In this scenario, one naturally wonders how privatisation will lead to quality boosting, as some people claim.

As per a survey conducted by NASSCOM, 20 per cent of the engineering colleges of the country are of 'ordinary' grade and 60 per cent are of second grade on international standards. A good number of these institutions are struggling with shortage of teachers. There is a dearth of qualified faculty and very few faculty with Ph.D. are available. On the parameters of resources and facilities, many institutions are in pitiable condition. Hardly any college of the country conducts real practical classes.

A large number of minority institutions have been opened in the name of vocational education. Judged on number, Hindu institutions are in minority in Kerala. Out of 150 engineering institutions, 110 are minority institutions. Commercialisation has assumed monstrous dimension in vocational and professional institutions. In the years 2006-2007, nine students committed suicide for this reason. U.R. Rao (Ex-Chairman, ISRO) Committee (2003) observed that expenditure on one engineering student is, on an average, ₹ 20 to 22 thousand. In Andhra Pradesh, the tuition fee is between ₹ 22 and 25 thousand, while the states of Rajasthan, Uttar Pradesh, Uttarakhand etc. charge anything between ₹ 60 and 70 thousand.

Vocational and Professional education has not even a distant relation with value based education. There is hardly any consideration of the national ethos and specific needs in identifying vocational courses and framing their curriculum. Many management institutes have got affiliation with foreign universities and have blindly adopted their curriculum in toto. While considering vocational education, NKC did not deem it worthwhile to think about Information Technology stream. In the last few years, the reputation of Bharat has moved very high because of our expertise in information technology. We have more than 2.5 lakh IT engineers, but this should not make us complacent. We also need to deliberate on the facts that we depend on America for our IT sector to flourish. We are way ahead in software, but we lag behind other developed countries in hardware. The blueprint of IT development of our country is not accordant to our requirements. In our local markets today, companies like IBM, ORACLE etc. are in greater demand.

National Knowledge Commission should have contemplated on issues like this in greater details. But what we actually experienced is that the Commission had neither persons in it capable of such a serious thinking, nor they appreciated such thoughts or required people to extend relevant suggestions. Two years earlier, very few people were familiar with National Knowledge Commission. It was ABVP, Bharatiya Shikshan Mandal, Vidya Bharati, Rashtriya Shaikshik Mahasangh, Shiksha Bachao Andolan etc. which organised a large number of seminars and symposia apropos NKC that publicised it. We also extended important suggestions. But the NKC, what to think of organising dialogue with such organisations, has not even responded to request from these organisations for a formal meeting.

The more important fact is that the recommendations of NKC hardly include in their basis any input from the common man, especially students. Those who participated in its decision-making appear to be persons subscribing to a specific school of thought. A conscious and deliberate attempt to keep at distance important organisations working in the education sector is highly unfortunate. In 1967, when New Education Policy was proposed, the Congress itself was in power at the centre, but it had invited institutions and organisations of all ideological hues for suggestions. But the NKC did not do anything like this. A question naturally arises—does the chairman of NKC wish to educate Bharat on the basis of trash collected from a chosen elite, while himself stationed in America? In the two reports so far tabled by NKC, educationists of the country are frantically searching 'knowledge', but so far they have found none!

—15 Dec, 2009

□

Restructuring of Curriculum: A Draft

The educational structure of the country should be compatible with its culture and ethos. In addition to this, it should fulfil national and societal requirements and should be able to contribute to the character building and holistic development of students' personality. The Delor's Commission of UNESCO has, in its report, deliberated in detail on the nature and structure of a country's education. The report concluded with an opinion that it should be compatible with the culture, ethos and progression of the country concerned. Similarly, in the opinion of renowned educationist Shri Dinanath Batra, 'education should be for living and life'.

In view of the nature of education discussed above, the following points need to be considered while developing a curriculum:

Curriculum should Incorporate Values

- There is no need of a separate book or a specific period of study or a specialised teacher for value education.
- There may be reference books for guidance of teachers.
- Elements of value should be included in the textbooks of all subjects.
- Relevant activities and programmes according to the level or standard of students are needed.
- With this purpose, in the courses of every faculty, at

the very outset, the social and national angle of the concerned faculty should be discussed with students.

Curriculum Should not be Merely Theoretical

- There should be harmonious balance between theory and practice or principles and their application.
- This attitude is required for curriculum right from primary classes up to higher education.

Other Important Elements

- The basis should be thoughts and pattern of the past, duly modified to meet the demands of the present and should combine a futuristic vision.
- Textbooks of all subjects should be available in the mother tongue and the medium of teaching at all levels should be a Bharatiya language.
- The opening chapter of every book should delineate the history of the concerned subject in Bharat.
- There should be an amalgamation of materialism with spiritualism and of the modern with the ancient.
- All distortions and contortions in the curriculum as well as textbooks through which our culture, tradition, religion and human icons are being denigrated and slandered, should be expunged outright.
- The contribution of Bharat to the world in the areas of knowledge and science should be essentially taught at all levels.
- Factually correct history of the country should be taught with an honest intention to make students take pride in their country and to inculcate in them love and honour for their country. The orientation of the teaching of history should be such that the young generation may take lesson from the errors committed in the past, lest they may recur.
- Special arrangement should be in place to enlighten

students moving abroad for studies, with rich culture, religion and traditions of Bharat.

Subjects for Holistic Development of Personality

The following subjects should be included, inter alia, in the main subjects of study with a view to evolve a balanced personality of the young learner:

1. Music; 2. Fine Arts; 3. Yoga; 4. Physical Education; 5. Sanskrit; 6. Vedic Mathematics; 7. Social Work.

Resolution of National and International Challenges and Fulfilment of Needs

The following subjects need to be included in curriculum to address major issues facing the world:

1. Terrorism and National Security.
2. Economic Imperialism and Global Recession.
3. Fusion of Science and Spiritualism.
4. Environment

Some Broad Measures for Restructuring of Curriculum

- Stiff regimentation of subjects within a faculty should be done away with.
- Curriculum should be reviewed at an interval of every three years.
- There should be a cohesion between national planning and educational planning. Curriculum should naturally emerge from this cohesion.
- Institutions for different faculties and streams should be opened to meet the specific needs of the country. With this purpose, manpower survey should be conducted in the country.
- Curriculum should be developed with due consideration of regional requirements. Rural and tribal areas should be meticulously focused in the curriculum.

Pursuit of education on the basis of such a balanced curriculum will lead to the making of a knowledgeable, skilled and service oriented youth. Only such youth may be capable of playing a positive role in fulfilling the needs of society and country, besides resolving the issues that the society and the nation are facing.

—2 June, 2020

□

The Notion of Self-Financing Institutions and their Role

The impact of globalisation began to sway Bharat since 1990, which also affected the education sector. This was followed by proliferation of private educational institutions. With increase of private institutions in number, commercialisation also began to be discussed all around. For colleges like this, special rules and provisions should be made, especially in the context of fee-structure, because they have become infamous for charging exorbitant fees. In general parlance, private institutions are aptly called 'self-financing institutions'.

Need of Self-Financing Institutions

The idea that entire education should be managed solely by the government, is neither proper nor practicable. During the last decate the enrolment of youth (between 14 and 23 years) in higher education increased from 7 to 12 per cent. This is co-synchronous with the increase in the number of self-financing institutions. The share of such institutions in developed countries is 40 per cent while in developing ones it is 24 per cent. In our country, there are 480 universities and about 22,000 colleges. As per an estimate made by the Ministry of Human Resource Development, in order to increase Gross Enrolment Ratio in higher education from a meagre 12% to 30%, we require 800 universities and 35,000 colleges in the country. In order to proceed further for realisation of the target, we will continue to add self-financing courses.

Present Scenario

The number of self-financing courses in the country is far less than what is required. The available institutions lag behind in educational standards. Most of them have become centres of business. The government is largely responsible for this. Their attitude towards such institutions has been very flexible. This is either intentional or due to a willing indifference to regulate them. The unbridled commercialisation of these institutions is tacitly aided and abetted by people in power. The arrest of the chairman of the Medical Council of India recently has exposed the role and connivance of the regulators sitting at the helm of the system. In some states, people in power have themselves opened many such institutes.

Consequences

In our country, education has been considered a means to serve the masses. But contrary to it, education has assumed the face of a business. It is clearly visible now that such institutions cater to students from the affluent section of society. The standard of teaching in these institutions is rapidly falling down. In many institutions, teachers themselves help students in using unfair means, besides copying in the examination. In order to attract students to their institution, such unfair measures are used. In some of these institutions, western model is blindly adopted in so-called cultural programmes in which uninhibited show of the skin is common. This has a harmful effect on the students' life. Our cultural heritage is also being damaged by this. In the self-financing institutions, there is also a tendency of exploitation of teachers by the management.

Remedy

The remedy lies in the hands of the stakeholders. Students, teachers, self-financing institutions and society need to work in tandem to correct the wrongs concerning these institutions.

The Role of the Government

It is not proper that the government should hand over higher education to the private parties and set itself free from its responsibility. For the last few years, the central and state governments have almost ceased to open new vocational institutes. In my humble opinion, at least 50 per cent of vocational institutions should be opened by the government and the remaining 50 per cent should be self-financing, otherwise children of only 15 to 20 per cent families of the country can get vocational education. Do the children of the remaining 80 per cent families not have merit to get vocational education? If these children are not given equal opportunity, their talent will be frustrated. The country will have to pay a heavy price for this.

The government should frame law to regulate self-financing institutions, which should prescribe a uniform fee-structure, pay-structure for teachers and standards of quality. The opening of such institutes, in the context of subject and location, should be allowed on the basis of actual academic and regional needs identified through manpower surveys. As similar parameters were not applied in opening new engineering colleges in Tamil Nadu, Andhra Pradesh, Maharashtra etc. especially those in rural areas, seats are remaining vacant and some colleges are on the verge of being closed. Persons with honest intent of service should come forward to open self-financing institutions. This needs to be encouraged by the government also.

The Role of Self-financing Institutions

Educational institutions may be self-financing but they cannot become a sourse of indiscriminate money-minting. With an eye on Bharatiya concept of education as a means of service to society, it should play this role and come upto the expectations of society. Those who are financially capable should pay higher fees. Making such arrangement will enable the institution to earn adequate money to run it smoothly. Every institution should fulfil national responsibility by granting free ship to 15 or 20 per cent of its students who are economically weak. The institutions should, instead of damaging Bharatiya culture, enrich it through suitable on-campus activities. There should be in these institutions economic righteousness, high academic standards, arrangements for holistic development of learners and efforts for sensitising students regarding their social responsibility. There should be a transparent democratic pattern in the academic administration of the institution.

The Role of Society

It had never been an assumption in Bharat that education is the sole responsibility of the government or the ruler. We believe that education is a responsibility of society. As such, prominent persons of society should come forward to open educational institutions. The society itself needs to play the role of regulatory authority for self-financing institutions. In the age of economic globalisation, better education justifies higher expenditure. However, it should always be at the back of our mind that giving education is a social service, never a business for profit. A universal awareness of and commitment to this vital truth need to be created.

—3 Nov, 2014

□

National Reconstruction and Education: Global Perspective

What is a Nation?

- It is written in the *Rig Veda*—माता भूमि: पुत्रोऽहं पृथिव्या:—'i.e. 'Earth is our mother and we are her children'.
- Where there is a defined piece of land inhabited by a community of people who have in their heart a feeling of boundless reverence for their motherland.
- That community of people has similar ideals of life.
- That community has a special vision to observe.
- That community has the same set of friend and foe.
- That community has similar sense of reverence for iconic persons of the past.
- The community follows the same tradition.
- The community has similar aspirations.

On the basis of the proposition as above, a certain culture evolves there, as it happened in our country.

What is a State?

- A state secures peace in society, removes distortions, if any, in social life, by simplifying the complexities entering the social system, ensures a just and dignified life to every individual and, thus, establishes order in society.

- A state establishes relation with other states.
- It saves its people from internal disturbance and external invasion.

What is a Country?

- Land and people taken together constitutes a country.
- Country is a visible entity, nation an invisible one.
- Unless a country exists, nation cannot be imagined.

National Reconstruction

The organisers have used the expression 'reconstruction' instead of 'new construction'. This is so because in the past days our nation was capable, affluent and accomplished from all angles and all the systems were of high order. Our elemental basis was spiritualism but we were affluent materialistically too. This was the reason foreign invaders attacked Bharat for sheer loot and plunder. The philosophical principles behind our systems and management are eternal truth which are still relevant for us. Therefore, a new system will have to be created in the light of those elemental principles having perennial relevance which could meet the needs of the modern society.

When we think of educational system in ancient Bharat, the image of *Gurukul* flashes in our mind. This may not be possible today, although some experiments may be done, and some experiments are actually underway. But essential notions and virtues of the ancient system which impress us are the ideal teacher—taught relation, a sense of family, and education as a mode of service rather than a gainful business. These are highly relevant even today. These notions and virtues of the ancient system will have to be adopted in the modern context.

Aim of Education

ॐ असतो मा सद्गमय, तमसो मा ज्योतिर्गमय, मृत्योर्माऽमृतं गमय।

"Ohm! Lead us from Unreality (of transitory existence) to the Reality (of the external self), lead us from the Darkness (of ignorance) to the Light (of spiritual knowledge), lead us from the Fear of Death to the Knowledge of Immortality".

This is the aim of education. There should be no difference between the aim of life and education.

Education means holistic development of students' personality and their character building. In broad perspective, education should facilitate the fulfilment of national requirements.

- **Swami Vivekananda:** The aim of education is to articulate the perfection inherent in man in nascent state.
- **Munshi Premchand:** That model of education which lacks concern for society and nation can never be deemed real education.
- **Dr. S. Radhakrishnan:** Our education will be deemed incomplete until it includes in it religious thoughts.
- **Dinanath Batra:** Education is for living and life.

Holistic Development of Student's Personality

Notion of Panchakosh in the Upanishad:

Annamay Kosh—Development of physical body

Pranamay Kosh—Development of Vital force

Manomay Kosh—Development of psyche

Vigyanmay Kosh—Development of wisdom and sensibility

Anandmay Kosh—Development of soul and spirituality

The meaning of the *koshas* given above are not exact and final. They just represent their significance in the nearest possible terms. However, their meaning in itself suggest in unmistakable terms that holistic development of a man can be achieved through the development, nourishment and enrichment of physical body, vital force, psyche, wisdom and soul. This enables a person to assume personality.

Sometime back, an article written by Ms. Kiran Bedi was published in a newspaper. She wrote that she had to deliver a speech in a public function. She was thinking about the subject on which she should speak. Many alternatives came to her mind but she finally chose the subject of character because, she thought, there was a scarcity of men of character in the country. This is a reality, a bitter truth, which is accepted by one and all. It is for lack of character in general that many problems and dangerous situations occurred in our country. In this context, a saying is highly relevant:

If wealth is lost, nothing is lost.
If health is lost, something is lost.
If character is lost, everything is lost.

It is necessary to think about a new concept of education in the light of the principle given above.

What should be the Practical Shape of Education based on Thoughts Explained Above

- Inclusion of values of life makes education value-based. This important input in every textbook is imperative in order to inculcate in students love for social service and feeling of patriotism which, together, will build their character in the right way. Social work should be made compulsory for students at all levels.
- Instead of making education merely theoretical, it should also include applied aspect of the subject. This is required at every level. Education should focus on labour, duty, skill development and creation of employment.
- Education should be a sensible amalgam of the ancient, the modern, the material and the spiritual elements.
- Education should be liberated from the clutches of administration and politics. With this purpose, an Autonomous Education Council should be formed at the national level with its branches or units at state and district levels.

For Fulfilling the Needs, and Addressing the Challenges of the Country and the World:

- Solution to the challenges of terrorism and national security should be an essential part of syllabus at all levels.
- Teaching of military science as a subject should be compulsory in school.
- Environmental conservation should be taught.
- There should be a combination of spiritual and scientific outlook in teaching.
- Teaching of health and hygiene should be included in curriculum.
- Teaching of yoga as a subject is useful.
- Education should promote research and investigation to address social and national issues.

Reconstruction or recreation of education in all its dimensions is fundamental as well as primary work. Great persons of the past wished to make the country capable, powerful, prosperous and to reclaim its lost seat as mentor of the world. Their wishes can be realised only when education is effectively regenerated.

—15 Nov, 2014

□

Bharatiya Languages: Issue of Existence and Honour

Bharatiya languages have had an important place in the contexts that give completeness to the diversity of Bharat, in the cultural elements which have conserved this feature of diversity for thousands of years, and in the cultural strands which rendered unique service towards making cultural unity of the country eternally and perennially intact. Reckless expansion of western culture have caused great damage to Bharatiya languages, culture, religion and society. But greater damage was caused under government's patronisation after Independence. We have no hesitation in asserting that the identity of Bharat was hurt in a planned way, and also that a sizeable section of society has been running a campaign under cover of an ideology to completely destroy this identity forever. A natural question arises in our mind as to why a conspiracy was planned by our own brethren to destroy that cultural identity of Bharat by dint of which we had gained supremacy in the world? Why the vast reservoir of Bharatiya languages, various dimensions of culture, religion and spiritualism which were highly acclaimed in the whole world were targeted for eating like termites? These are not mere questions. These are the alarming signals of a crisis which need to be analysed in its depth and dimensions.

All those who invaded Bharat, injured our cultural identity. First of all, the Mughals made every attempt to crush, through their dictatorial rule, our linguistic, cultural and religious unity. They were also successful to a certain extent. Afterwards, the Britons also followed the same course in this context. In some issues, they proved more dangerous than the Mughals. From the facts delineated above, a question arises as to what have we and our people done since Independence to save the Bharatiya languages to conserve our cultural identity and to enrich our cultural heritage?

After Independence, when the proposal of one Bharatiya language along with regional languages surfaced, English, surprisingly, emerged as a more important language. The entire proposal was twisted in favour of English in such a way that instead of arriving at a solution of the language issue, a controversy was generated on linguistic lines leading to clash of interest among ethnic groups of the country. The issue of language was made a matter of regional and political controversy. Was this itself our Independence? Was this itself the thing for which our ancestors fought a long battle? Our opposition is not to English or any other foreign language. We are opposed to the vicious minds which are bent on wiping out the honour and identity of Bharatiya languages.

Bharat is a country of villages. Villages have been the progenitors and foster hubs of Bharatiya culture. Bharatiya languages have also been patronised more by the villages. Therefore, in order to save and enrich Bharatiya languages and the cultures linked to each language, it preconditions special discussion of cultural rejuvenation of villages. For linking regional and provincial languages with literature, society, education, judiciary and technology, initiative should be begun, first of all, by creating mass awareness and, secondly, by concrete efforts of the government. I personally believe that we should not expect the government to accomplish it all alone. This task may be accomplished more conveniently through coordinated effort of government and people representing society. The truth is visible to all of us that development, upliftment and regeneration of society has always been possible through coordination of peoples' participation and governmental support. Once again we have to make positive efforts for upliftment of the nation to the best of our capacity. For this, it is necessary that a well-planned scheme should be devised to enable the collective mind of the masses to express itself in its natural language. This requires efforts at two levels. Firstly, the medium of instruction should be the language of the respective states of the country. In the existing arrangement regarding language, even in Hindi-speaking states, English is used simultaneously with state language. This arrangement needs to be modified. The ideal arrangement would be that education, administration and justice should use the mode of the language of the state. At the central level, education, administration and justice should use the mode of Bharatiya language. Only this can ensure both equality in, and sovereignty of, the nation. Work at the primary level in the states with regard to education, administration and justice is done, to some extent, in the language of the state, but as soon as the issues move to higher level or if some national issues come under discussion, the language invariably changes to English. The students' education in the medium of the language of their states have to face embarrassment and discrimination later because the medium of teaching and learning in higher education, and the language of interaction in the higher section of society, is usually English. In such a situation, which parents will not like their wards to learn English so that they have smooth upward movement in education and social life. This is the reason the general masses are in a fix regarding Bharatiya languages.

This may be a right issue for consideration, discussion and differences of opinion, but the focal point, instead of being its causality, should be a way out of this and its ideal solution. People's aspiration supported by political will can help realise an ideal shape of things. An important thing to be noted in this context is that these arguments are not focused on opposition of English but our sane intention is to put an end to that mentality which is creating two separate Bharat in the country. For equity of citizens, it is necessary to have one language at the national level. Hence a positive initiative in this direction is highly imperative, so that we can move forward on the right path in a healthy ambience of equality and brotherhood.

—13 July, 2016

□

Mother Tongue

In the present times, when language has become a subject of popular discussion, on the other side of it, the significance of mother tongue appears to be diminishing. The conclusion of about 150 studies in the world over last 40 years has been that education should be given through mother tongue because a child begins to imbibe the *sanskar* of mother tongue since his existence in his mother's womb. Bharatiya scientist, C.V. Shrinath Shastri experienced that students having read engineering in the medium of Bharatiya languages are more adept in scientific investigation than those read in English medium. As per a research of Dr. Nandini Singh of National Brain Research Centre, Gurugram, during the process of reading English, only one side of the brain becomes active, whereas during the process of reading Hindi, both sides of the brain become active. Isaac Pitman, who developed the signs of shorthand, asserted that if there is a fully developed, perfect script in the world, it is Devnagari. Learning through a foreign language is also inconsistent with the principles of modernity, because modern knowledge can be propagated in society only through their own language.

This also is a fact that Hindi is being taught, in one way or the other, in about 170 countries of the world. Sanskrit is being taught in more than 32 universities of the world. In Saint James School of England, learning Sanskrit is compulsory upto class 6. In Bharat also, wherever there was opposition of Hindi, for political reasons of course, and where Hindi was used very little, as in the states of Tamil Nadu, Mizoram, Nagaland etc. now Hindi speaking classes have opened on popular demand. In Arunachal Pradesh, Hindi is the language of public communication and in Nagaland, Hindi is the second state language. A large number of candidates take examinations conducted by Dakshin Hindi Prachar Sabha, Madras Rashtrabhasha Prachar Samiti, M.G. International Hindi University, Wardha etc. In fact, Bharatiya languages have no challenge from English, but only from the Bharatiyas with English mindset. We do not have to advocate for Hindi or any particular language of Bharat . But we do have to advocate in this regard, for a scientifically and logically sound principle in the interest of the nation.

Mother tongue is easy to learn and comprehend. As such, transfer of knowledge is smooth in the medium of mother tongue. Former President, Dr. Abdul Kalam stated what he experienced as a student, "I became a successful scientist because I received the education of science and mathematics in the medium of mother tongue (at Dharampeth College, Nagpur)". For learning through English, a student is required to put in extra labour. For pursuing medical or engineering courses, one has to learn English first, and then he can acquire knowledge of one's core subject. Madan Mohan Malaviya was a scholar of English. English scholars came to listen to his English, but he had said, "I have been using English for 60 years, but speaking English is not as smooth as Hindi". Likewise, Rabindranath Thakur opined, "If science is to be made accessible to the common man, it should be taught in the medium of mother tongue." Mahatma Gandhi observed, "The medium of foreign language has burdened the child's faculties, compels them to learn by rote and, as a result they fail to become creative. Foreign language has also constrained the growth of Bharatiya languages."

In the economically and intellectually developed countries

like America, Russia, China, Japan, Korea, England, France, Britain, Germany, Spain, Israel etc. their own languages are the medium of education as well as administration. Sixteen scholars of Israel received Nobel Prize. All of them worked in their mother tongue, Hebrew. A retired senior scientist of Microsoft, Sankrant Sanu stated in his book that top twenty countries of the world on the basis of Gross Domestic Product (GDP) were executing all their work in their own languages. Only four of these work in English because it is their mother tongue. He wrote further that twenty countries at the bottom of this ranking use English, or a mix of English and their own language, in higher education and administration. The import of his observation is that unless and until the medium of education, competitive examination, administration, judiciary etc. does not become our own language, our country cannot progress.

According to Shri Pradip Joshi, former Diretcor of National Institute of Educational Planning and Administration (NIEPA), the world-famous nuclear scientist and Vice Chancellor of Hiroshima University of Japan does not know English. In our country, a logic is put forward that in this globalised system, the knowledge of English is necessary for studying or working in a foreign country. About two lakh persons go to foreign countries from Bharat every year. All of them do not go to English speaking countries. For the benefit of only this much of people, imposing English on crores of students isn't an act of injustice and atrocity? However, learning a new language is not difficult. Any language can be learnt in three to six months. On the other hand, the knowledge stored in other languages of the world are not available to us because we do not think of any other foreign language beyond English. The books of science are abundant in Russian and German languages. Likewise, books of German philosophers are available in German and those of literature, poetry and archaeology in French.

One more logic is given that books for higher education, especially in the streams of science and technology are not available in our native languages. It is not difficult to translate a book in other languages into ours. But our mindset is such that we consider books in English as best, and serve our purpose by copying from them. Very little work is being done in our country to produce the required books based on original thoughts and academic research in this direction. We are not aware of our virtues and specialities. The successfully organised Kumbh Fair of Prayag or Tiffin Distribution System of Mumbai are instances of smart management. When people from abroad came to study their brilliant management, the scholars of Bharatiya Management Institutes became aware of their significance.

Most of the renowned scientists of Bharat received their education in their mother tongue. Important among these are Jagdish Chandra Bose, Shrinivasa Ramanujan and Dr. A.P.J. Abdul Kalam. Likewise, most of the students obtaining high marks in the examinations of school level boards of states also learned through the medium of their own language. Various commissions on education and eminent persons of the country recommended that mother tongue should be the medium of education. Mahatma Gandhi aptly said, "Mother tongue is as much necessary for children's mental development as mother's milk for their physical development".

English education for the last 175 years has caused great damage to the nation, and the damage continues. The mind of children is unnecessarily burdened by English. This is a sort of atrocity on them. Therefore, their mental development is not coming about properly. They can learn neither English nor their mother tongue properly. This results in wastage of time, labour and resources. Education is not becoming universal and all-inclusive. In our country, students in greatest number fail in English and mathematics. The medium of a foreign language can enable us to get some information or knowledge but it cannot beget creative knowledge. In the same way, we are lagging behind in research work. Research work and writings in the country are done mostly in English. Hence, instead of people of our country, foreigners are reaping their greater benefit. The scholars of our country are becoming dependent on foreign countries.

In our country today, English is the language of the upper section of society while Bharatiya languages are spoken and used by the rest of the people. This has created two separate classes. Of all the foreign languages, we learn only English. Therefore, we observe the whole world from English vision. In fact, to understand the world better and to develop a good relation with important countries of the world, we need to learn eight languages at the least—Russian, Chinese (Mandarin), Japanese, Spanish, German, English, Arabic and French. The importance and currency of English is more in those countries which had been under British dominion. Other countries are according greater importance to their own language. It is only Bharat which is unnecessarily bearing the load of slavery at its own will.

In view of the present state of things, there seems no exaggeration in the opinion that English has become a language of exploitation. About 95 per cent people of Bharat cannot understand the communications made in English in the sector of medicine, engineering, judiciary and administration. Books published in the country in English have a turnover of more than ₹ 2000 crore per year.

People speaking French, German and Japanese aggregate to a meagre two per cent, but they command considerable respect in the world. While people speaking Hindi are more than 70 crore, yet the world looks down upon us. The instances of assault of Bharatiya students in America and Australia point towards the world's attitude towards us.

Language is a carrier and conductor of culture and *sanskar*. Dying out of Bharatiya languages is leading to decadence of culture. With change in language, a change in values also sets in invisibly. Language is the abode of culture. In Finland, Swedish language was used some 100 years ago and in Russia, during the reign of the Czars, French language enjoyed supremacy. In both these countries, by dint of strong will-power of the people and the rulers, their native languages are now used in all sectors. In our country also a similar will-power needs to be developed in its people. We can very well begin with ourselves. Let us begin to do our own and our organisation's work in our own language. We may admit our children in schools teaching in our language. The signboards and nameplates of our houses, offices and organisations should be written in our language. In our personal letters, official applications, invitation cards we should be particular to use our own language.

This is a long-lasting battle. Hence we should make concerted effort. First of all, we should remove the illusion regarding utility of English and re-establish Bharatiya language at the scientifically and logically assigned seat of honour through extensive public awareness programmes by way of seminars, workshops and dialogues. Secondly, research centres will have to be set up for carrying out research and production of creative literatures in various Bharatiya languages. Wherever and whenever the government violates the provisions of language act or demeans Bharatiya languages in any way, we will have to fight to stop this and fight legal battle if required. Parliamentarians and political groups having love and respect for Bharatiya languages should be brought to a common platform and make efforts for a comprehensive debate in the parliament on the issue of languages. Hindi and Bharatiya languages, apart from being made the medium of instruction, also need to be linked to job. Work in the Supreme Court should be conducted in Hindi and in the High Courts, it should be in the language of the state and the Raj Bhasha of the country. With this purpose, advocates with a feeling for languages should be brought to a common platform. Students should initiate organised struggle for removing English as a compulsory subject and replace it with Hindi and other Bharatiya languages. In order to initiate all these actions, all language loving citizens, social and political organisations, institutions and NGOs will have to be united on a common platform for pushing the struggle further, and until the end is achieved. This is an undebatable truth that Bharatiya languages will finally win.

—17 Jan, 2019

□

International Mother Tongue Day: 21st February

21st February is celebrated as International Mother Language Day. In 1952, on this very day, students of Dhaka University, Jagannath University and Medical College of Bangladesh (then East Pakistan) were subjected to police firing in their agitation for declaring Bangla language as state language. Many students became martyrs for the sake of their mother tongue. To commemorate their sacrifice for mother tongue, UNESCO, in 1999, began to celebrate the day as 'International Mother Language Day', which was approved by UNO in 2008.

According to UNESCO, language, instead of being a sheer medium of communication, education or development, is a unique identity of a person and a treasure of his culture, tradition and history. To highlight this significance of language, UNESCO observed the year 2019 as the 'Year of Native Languages'. About the importance of mother tongue, UNESCO says that it is necessary for knowledge, peace, rights, inclusion and variety. Every language carries with itself a unique tradition of knowledge and by aiding the development process of the country promotes all-round peace. It grants to the people of a country the fundamental right to education and ensures inclusiveness of all sections of the society. Thus, mother tongue also performs the task of putting together the heritage of cultural values of society.

Some scholars believe that mother's language itself is mother tongue. This is not complete truth. Along with mother's language, the place where a child's childhood and adolescence is spent, its ambience has mother's aura. The surroundings in which children grow and the language they learn there becomes their mother tongue. Here surroundings include the child's family and the family's cultural values.

There are many popular illusions is our country regarding language. The prominent illusion is that English is the language of development. This is so despite the fact that UNESCO and many other institutes have proved in their investigation that a child's education in his own language facilitates his real growth. Hence, education in the medium of mother tongue is a perfect scientific proposition. The National Brain Research Centre and Commissions related to education also endorse this view. Bharatiya scientist C.V. Shrinath Shastri has the experience that students having pursued engineering course in the medium of Bharatiya languages are cabable of doing better scientific research than those having pursued their course in the English medium.

Mahatma Gandhi had said, "Medium of foreign language has burdened the faculties of children, and compelled them to memorise, instead of promoting their creativity. Foreign language has hampered the growth of native languages." In this context, Dr. A.P.J. Abdul Kalam, former President of Bharat and a great scientist opined, "I could become a successful scientist because I had learnt science and mathematics through my mother tongue". Similarly, a retired senior scientist of Microsoft, Sankrant Sanu, worte in his book that the top twenty countries in the ranking on the basis of GDP do all their work in their native languages, and only four in this group work in English because it is their mother tongue. He further writes that twenty countries at the bottom of this ranking work either in a foreign language, or mix their native language with a foreign language in higher education, and in governance and administration too, the same language policy is followed. When we compare the number of Nobel laureates of India with that of the countries giving education in their native languages, like Israel, Japan, Germany etc. the picture becomes pretty clear and observations made above are proved beyond any doubt.

Despite immense significance of indigenous languages, we are lagging way behind in terms of enrichment of our languages. According to the findings of the People's Linguistic Survey of Bharat conducted in 2010, there are 780 languages in our country. They expressed the possibility of 100 more languages in existence. The languages like Vadari and Kolhati of Maharashtra, Golla and Gosari of Karnataka and Telangana etc. are some examples whose speakers being less than ten thousand in number, have been kept outside the master list. They have identified languages like Adhuni, Dichi, Ghallu, Helgo, Baa etc. which have become extinct.

Out of 197 languages on the verge of extinction in Bharat, only Bodo and Maitai enjoy official status because they have their own writing system. In a country like Bharat where the tradition of knowledge has usually been orally transferred to successive generations, the policy of not counting a language in the official list simply because some of them do not have a writing system, is completely divorced from historical and cultural realities of the country. Many languags are becoming extinct because of this faulty policy. The government of Bharat should review such erroneous rules without any delay so that in the census of 2021, such errors may be rectified and a realistic census could take effect.

Mother tongue is a prerequisite of not only acquisition of knowledge, but also of human rights protection, establishment of peace, social cohesion and persistent growth. However, foreign languages also have their importance for social, economic and political development, peaceful co-existence and social harmony. Many Bharatiya languages are facing the danger of extinction. We do not appear to be capable of enrichment of our languages and dialects, despite our faith in, and strength of, the variety of our culture. Considering these facts, inter alia, the UNO declared 2019 as the year dedicated to conservation and enrichment of indigenous languages.

—16 April, 2019

□

Bharatiya Languages in Judiciary

On 14th September, 1949 Hindi was made state language of the Union of Bharat. It is a matter of pride that Hindi, a language of the common man was, for the first time, constitutionally accredited as state language of the country. After Independence, states were re-organised on linguistic basis. Fourteen important languages of the country were enlisted in the 8th Schedule of the Constitution, which has now increased to 22.

Nonetheless, it is unfortunate that Hindi, the state language of the country, is not recognised by the Supreme Court. Similarly, no state, except four, has its state language recognised in the High Court. Is it a genuine democracy? This question naturally arises. The official language of those deprived states are also the language of the masses. Then depriving the state language from recognition in the High Court is sheer injustice. One reason of this may be that the Official Language Act-1963 enacted by the union government provided that English could continue to be used for official work until 26th January, 1965. Despite the lapse of this grace period, the Supreme and High Courts continued to use English in their official work. In another provision of this act, it was added that the Governor of the state, with consent of the President of Bharat, could permit the High Court to use in their official work Hindi and/or the official language of the state along with English. In exercise of this provision, the High Courts of Bihar, Rajasthan, Uttar Pradesh and Madhya Pradesh are doing legal work in Hindi.

The states like Jharkhand, Uttarakhand and Chhattisgarh, which were created after bifurcation of states mentioned earlier, should have automatically implemented their language policy in their High Courts, but this is yet to be done. As per States Reorganisation Act, when a state is bifurcated into two, the arrangements under major policies of the erstwhile united state are continued in the new entity also. But the governments of these newly formed states have not taken cognisance of this fact. Hence, in the High Courts of these three new states, their official language is not recognised.

When the states of Tamil Nadu, Gujarat and Chhattisgarh demanded the use of their official language in their High Courts as per the provision of the Official Languages Act 1963, the central government sought the opinion of the Chief Justice of the Supreme Court. The latter responded in the negative, and this was conveyed to the states under reference. It is highly intriguing in view of the fact that since the contextual law empowers the Governor of the state to implement, with the President's consent, the said provision on its own, then why was the opinion of the Chief Justice of Bharat asked for? Under the excuse of the disapproval of the Chief Justice of the Supreme Court, these three states were denied this privilege. This is sheer injustice. In a way, the central government violated the provisions enshrined in the Constitution.

Judicial system with its elaborate machinery was created in the country with the purpose that the common people should enjoy right to live with justice in every aspect and they should get justice when there is an unjust action against them. But the language in which our courts transact their business is beyond comprehension of 97 per cent people of the country. The language in which the judgement is handed over to them is an alien language which they cannot understand. From the angle of language, the higher judiciary exists only for three per cent of the population who can comprehend English. An absurd excuse given against using state specific language in High Courts is that the judges appointed on transfer from other states will have difficulty in working in the state's language. But the reality is that there are not even ten per cent of the total judges from outside the state. Usually, a maximum of two or three judges in the high courts are from other states. When the arguments in a certain case are to be made in a local language, the judges of the state can hear them. In the parliament, there is a system in place by which speech delivered in any language can be heard in the listener's own language through instantaneous translation. In the 24 High Courts and the Supreme Court, this system of translation can be adopted. Officers of national civil and police services have to learn the language of the state where they are posted. Similar arrangement should be made for judges also.

In the context of higher judiciary, there may be some difficulty in working in local languages, but in their subordinate outfits at district level, there are no judicial officers from other states. Besides, Criminal Procedure Code-272 and Civil Procedure Code-137 mandate the judicial work in district courts to be done in the respective language of the state. Still in many states, work is being transacted in English either partially or wholly. Many courts do not have typists and stenographers to work in local language. As a result, the arguments may be given and heard in local language but the judgement is written and typed in English. In many courts, arguments are also given in English. It appears that people in power are conspiring to keep the common man deprived of their right to get judicial work done in their language and justify their inaction by flimsy alibi.

In many states, their acts are also framed in English and some of them, not all, are translated into the language of the state. In fact, people in power do not want Bharatiya languages to gain a dignified position. This fact is proved in our experience. Shiksha Sanskriti Utthan Nyas has, in the last two years, filed about two thousand representations with the central and state governments against violation of Official Languages Act by them. Some of these yielded positive result.

But some states and their offices did not even follow the courtesy of giving a response.

In some states, the medium of legal education is English. Some are shifting to English from other languages. The government has established Law Universities which use English as medium of teaching. In competitive examination for judicial services also, similar situation is prevalent. Unless and until compulsory status of English is reviewed in administration, higher education, competitive examinations and judiciary, it is impossible to establish Bharatiya languages at prime position. With this purpose, a big campaign and movement is direly needed. Shiksha Sanskriti Utthan Nyas has initiated the process. Now it is required that thousands of institutions, scholars, language-lovers etc. should come to one platform and raise their collective voice to give a nationwide dimension to their efforts. Only such an aggressive attempt will make the deaf hear. Only this can lead to Bharatiya languages being used in administration, teaching at all levels, judiciary and competitive examinations. We call upon all people to join us in this nationwide movement to beget the Bharatiya languages the justice denied so far. Let us commit ourselves to this cause, we pray.

—3 Nov, 2014

□

Hindi as Global Language

Hindi became the official language of the country in 1949. Since then, Hindi has seen many ups and downs, yet it is continuously moving forward in the whole world. Now Hindi is not confined to Bharat only, but it has expanded to about 130 countries. Hindi is the official language of Fiji also, besides being recognised as a regional language in Mauritius, Trinidad, Guyana and Surinam. Apart from this, a large number of Hindi-speaking persons inhabit in countries like USA, UK, South Africa, Australia, New Zealand, Germany, Singapore, Canada, UAE etc. Judged on the number of speakers, Hindi is a language spoken by the largest number of people of the world. Although *Wikipedia* gives third position to Hindi after Mandarin (Chinese) and English, Dr. Jayanti Prasad Nautiyal has proved in his research that Hindi is at the first position. In this age of Science, it is a bitter irony that a vast country like Bharat has no definitive information regarding the number of speakers of its official language. According to the census of 2001, about 25.79 crore people used Hindi as their mother tongue, while according to the census of 2011, about 42.20 crore people used it as one of more than 50 dialects. As per a study of *'Ethnologue: Langauges of the World'*, the ranking of Hindi is second in the world, next only to Mandarin (Chinese). According to the study, the number of persons using Hindi as theis mother tongue, is about 37 crore and that of persons using it as their second language is about 12 crore. The number of people speaking Hindi as mother tongue is more than those speaking English and Spanish, by 34 and 35 crore respectively. The number of people speaking Mandarin is about 87 crore, but this is unjust that while Mandarin includes in it its subsidiary languages and dialects, Hindi is considered separate from its ancillary languages and dialects like Rajasthani, Marwari, Maithili, Awadhi, Brajbhasha etc. It is wrong and unjust to apply different parameters for two prominent languages of the world.

Five Hindi newspapers published from Bharat—*Dainik Bhaskar, Dainik Jagaran, Amar Ujala, Hindustan* and *Rajasthan Patrika*—are included in the first twenty newspapers of the world. In about 170 countries of the world, Hindi is taught in one way or the other. Moscow (Russia) is considered to be an important centre of the world for teaching and learning Hindi. Teaching and learning Hindi is done in Moscow Government University and two other universities of the country, where courses for B.A., M.A. and Ph.D. are offered. In the Jawaharlal Nehru Cultural Centre of Bharatiya Embassy in Russia, Hindi is taught free. There is such a school also in Moscow where children are taught Hindi from class VI. Russian scholars have been translating in Russian many dictionaries and textbooks of Hindi, besides authoring books in Hindi. A professor of St. Petersburg Govt. University, Moscow had a new Hindi textbook for Russian students prepared by them, released in the third International Regional Hindi Conference.

In the universities of Harvard, Yale, Chicago, Washington, Montana, Texas, California, Johns Hopkins and many others of the USA, courses in Hindi are offered. Many government schools of the USA are offering their students an option to learn Hindi. Besides these, Australian National University and Tokyo University are also offering courses in Hindi. In China, Hindi is taught in Pecking and Guadong universities. In the Gurukul School of Beijing also, Hindi is taught. In a country of the Far East, Fiji, Hindi is a compulsory subject at school level. In the Hindi Department of University of Delhi, a number of foreign students, in a large number from Japan and Korea, are seeking admission, lured by the prospect of lucrative placement in multi-national companies operating from Bharat.

In the wake of Bharat's growing economic, political and military ascendancy, the eagerness to learn the official language of Bharat, Hindi, is increasing fast in the world. To meet the requirements in this context, the government of Bharat set up World Hindi Secretariat in Mauritius in its first step towards establishing Hindi as a global language. This secretariat publishes international Hindi journal and newspaper. To establish Hindi on the global platform, some more efforts are required, especially to create a new, scientific font in Hindi that could be conveniently used by the new generation which is technically savvy. In addition to this, it is required to promote original writing aimed at young generation, and to make suitable arrangement for training foreigners and Bharatiya diaspora abroad in Hindi language.

The status and honour of Hindi in the global scenario is improving day by day but in its homeland, it is struggling with various hardships. Some time back in Bengaluru, a violent protest was staged by some politically motivated people against writing notices on Metro train stations in Hindi language. Such protests create linguistic dichotomy in society, besides making an atmosphere of opposition to official language of the country. We should not forget that Hindi is the official language of the country and this is a duty of every citizen to respect it. The official languages of states as well as that of the country need equal respect. It is unfortunate that such linguistic disputes are fomented to satisfy political interest. The need of the time is that all Bharatiya languages should stand in favour of one another. Country should be integrated through the variety of languages, rather than breaking it on this account.

In order to patronise a language, it is necessary to make it the medium of instruction from the stage of primary education to that of higher education. The waxing shadow of globalisation on the country's educational system is steadily diluting the practice of imparting education in the medium of either Hindi or mother tongue. In primary education, however, there exists some option of Hindi or mother tongue as medium of teaching and learning, but in higher education English has become the sole option. In about 150 studies conducted in the last 40 years, it has unanimously been concluded that education should be given in mother tongue only because the *sanskar* of mother tongue is acquired by the baby since his presence in the mother's womb. Dr. A.P.J. Abdul Kalam, the renowned scientist, acknowledged that it was because of his school education in the medium of mother tongue that he could become a good scientist.

In the higher education system of the country, around 60 lakh students from outside the cities get admitted but they fail to adjust with English language pervading the campus. Because of this discrepancy between the preferred language of the learner and that of education, higher education is falling short of achieving its objectives. Many other discrepancies can be seen in higher education. The entrance test of the Faculty of Law of University of Delhi in conducted in English despite the fact that the annual examination at the close of academic year has the option of English or Hindi to write the answer. This arrangement is beset with incongruities. When students of the languages other than English have already been filtered out at the entrance level, what purpose does the option of Hindi in annual examination serve? Moreover, the medium of teaching in this faculty is English and study materials are also in English only, then what is the justification of the option of Hindi for annual examination? The National Law Universities, which are the apex institutions in this faculty, also follow the same practice. Similarly, teaching of vocational courses are also conducted in English, and English alone. In most of the states, mainstream courses at higher education level follow the medium of English.

At the global level and inside the country, the use of Hindi is expanding fast but in education from primary to university level, the relevance of Hindi and other Bharatiya languages is simultaneously shrinking. The number of students learning through the medium of Hindi and other Bharatiya languages is steadily falling. In fact, all the studies regarding language conducted inside and outside the country point towards one unanimous opinion that mother tongue should be the medium of instruction. Mahatma Gandhi had also said that our children spend at least six years on learning English but if they utilise it for learning the subjects of their study, they will acquire much more knowledge of their subjects.

All administrative work of the country is being done mostly in English. The medium of competitive examination is either English or a paper in English language has been made compulsory. In most of the courts of law, business is transacted in English. Unless and until the challenges facing Hindi and Bharatiya languages are not solved, their position cannot improve. The Official Languages Act 1963 and relevant orders of the President in this regard should be strictly complied with. The medium of primary level teaching must be the child's mother tongue. At the level of higher education, the options of Hindi and Bharatiya languages should be made available along with English. For development of Hindi and Bharatiya languages, every state should establish a university dedicated to their state language. English should no longer be compulsory in competitive examinations.

Countrywide campaigns should be launched at social level to ensure honour, development of, and people's sense of pride in the Bharatiya languages. With these efforts only, Bharatiya languages can develop and Hindi can gain the status of world language.

—2 July, 2018

□

All India Services: The Issue of Language

A professional service like Indian Information Service was included in the general Civil Services Examination, although this service was created as a specialised service in 1959.

All Bharatiya services have a special status because these are linked to the future of lakhs of meritorious students, besides the administrative structure of the country is based on these. But in many aspects, they appear to be the prototypes of the ICS of the British period. Decades after Independence, the government had constituted Basawan Committee to look into the state of these services. The recommendations of this committee reveal some important aspects of Bharatiya civil services. The important questions raised by the committee are—is this system of selection really competent to select suitable candidates for Bharatiya services, why should there not be separate examinations for specialists and generalists, are the eligibility criteria fixed for services in Group-A and B justified and compatible with the concerned services? The answer to most of these questions are in the negative. Recently, the C-SAT part of the Civil Services Examination was withdrawn under direct interference of the parliament. This proves our stand that there are many shortcomings in the selection procedure which need to be set right. Lack of compatibility amongst nature, requirement and eligibility of, and for, the services is visible to naked eyes. Examinations for Bharatiya Engineering and Economic/Statistical Services are conducted separately but the examination for Indian Information service is mixed with general Civil Service Examination. In this age of revolution in information sector—when it has come to be popularly accepted that 'Information is power'—this is globally deemed the most potent mode of empowerment in the whole world. But in our country, the service related to the information network is not in proper, professional shape. Hence, it becomes Imperative to discuss the incongruities in the composition of Indian Information Service. Since 1959, when this service was conceived, it began as a professional outfit comprising of only personnel with training and experience in the field of journalism. In 1987, this arrangement was vertically changed when professional journalists were deprived from the opportunity to serve in this service and general graduates were made eligible by including it in the Civil Service Examination conducted by UPSC. This step considerably weakened the professionalism of the service which is visible in the insufficient transmission of information regarding popular schemes of the government to its beneficiaries at the lowest rung of the pyramid. The irony in the conception of the service is that the service is divided in Group 'A' and 'B'. In Group 'B', which is an inferior cadre, professionals with degree and three years' experience are eligible, whereas in Group 'A', which is a superior cadre, generalists with simple graduate degree in any discipline become eligible. This leads to an unwelcome reality, in which the experience and understanding of the subject of the junior personnel is superior to that of the senior personnel.

An analysis of the educational background of the 162 personnel of Information Service made public by the government presents a curious picture. Out of 162 personnel, 89 were from Humanities, 27 from Science, 16 from Engineering, 14 from Management and 5 each from Commerce, Law and Medical background. No personnel from journalism background figured in this data. The extent of problems regarding such professional services can be gauged from an extract of the report of Satish Chandra Committtee formed to advise on reformation of civil services—"Some Group—A services like Indian Defence Estates Service, Indian Trade service, Indian Information Service etc. are not getting adequate officers etc. because these services do not figure in the preference list of candidates. Therefore, these services should be de-linked from Civil Services Examination". This is strange that in most of the states, the eligibility for appointment as Public Relation Officer is a degree in Journalism & Mass Communication, but it is not so in the central government. A natural result of this absurdity is that senior positions in broadcast agencies and the position of senior Public Relation Officers are manned by non-professional persons. Because of faulty policy in posting and promotion also, capable persons fail to get right position. In such a situation, the whole administrative system depends on Public Relation Agencies and media personnel appointed on contract. All Bharatiya services like this need to be brought to a proper shape and quality because these are broadly related to common people.

—15 Oct, 2018

□

Sanskrit vs. German Language

निज भाषा उन्नति अहे सब उन्नति को मूल।

बिन निज भाषा ज्ञान के मिटे न हिए का शूल॥

(भारतेंदु हरिश्चंद्र)

Promotion of our language, base of all development;

Without knowledge of own language, agony of heart won't die.

(Bharatendu Harishchandra)

In the present world, dark clouds are eclipsing the existence of different languages. Hundreds of languages have become gradually extinct. Many countries are being subjected to cultural invasion in the name of globalisation. Language is an important component of any culture. Language is not merely a mode of communication, but also a carrier of culture.

In the deluge of so-called globalisation, many languages are approaching their imminent extinction. In the past years, Bharat also witnessed a shrewd machination in this direction. In schools of Kendriya Vidyalaya Sangathan, Sanskrit was taught since 2011 under Three-language Policy. But surprisingly, Sanskrit was substituted by German language under an MoU with Goethe Institute. This was an illegal action because KVS had no right or power to sign such a contract. Shiksha Bachao Andolan launched a protest against this. When all efforts under democratic mode proved of no avail, the Sanskrit Teachers' Organisation filed a PIL in the Delhi High Court. The court's verdict pronounced on 15th October,

2014 was in favour of the petitioners. The then government at the centre was compelled to file an affidavit pledging to rectify the wrong action of KVS and to re-introduce Sanskrit in the schools. The MoU with the German organisation was not allowed to be renewed after end of its term.

The court's order as above and government's compliance thereof were vehemently opposed by some English newspapers and TV news channels and a lot of ruckus was created alleging the central Govt. of causing so-called harm to students by depriving them an opportunity to learn a foreign language which is highly relevant in this era of globalisation. It was also alleged that through re-introduction of Sanskrit, the government was advancing the agenda of saffronisation. Reading and listening to all this, the thought naturally came to mind that so much hullabaloo may not have been created even in Germany against withdrawal of German language from the curriculum. We simply have a sense of pity for the segment of media sponsoring such protest and, on the other hand, we feel natural anger against their anti-national conduct.

In accordance with the Education Policy-1986, three-language formula was implemented in the country. Its import was that students from classes 6 to 8 should be taught three languages. The three languages were to be chosen from amongst those Bharatiya languages enlisted in the 8th Schedule of the constitution. According to the Resolution (*sankalp*) adopted in both Houses of the Parliament on 18th January, 1968, in Hindi-speaking areas, one modern South Bharatiya language in addition to Hindi and English, while in non-Hindi speaking areas, a regional language in addition to Hindi and English was to be taught. It was also resolved that suitable arrangements were to be made for teaching of all such languages.

When in 2011, contrary to the country's education policy and the spirit of country's constitution, Sanskrit was substituted by German in an unlawful manner, a section of the media remained conspicuously silent but when this unlawful act was corrected, the same set of media and the so-called seculars began baseless protest. There cannot be a greater instance of misfortune for the country than this. The government has now set up a committee to probe such contracts having been signed in violation of law.

Friends! This is not meant to oppose German or any other language. But when the spirit of the Constitution or the country's education policy were wilfully violated with ulterior motive, the action must be opposed. Another important fact is that, in this age of globalisation, or without any consideration of this, if our students learn any foreign language, why should we have any objection to this? But in place of teaching Sanskrit, the mother of all languages, a foreign language is never acceptable to us. The third important fact is that our policy makers, educationists and citizens of the country should, instead of soaring high in the name of globalisation, keep their feet grounded on earth and adopt only those things which are strictly relevant to us. Today our students can learn any language of the world easily because our foundation is sound. The strong base of our languages is Sanskrit. If we shake this foundation, the structure erected on it will get damaged. The need of the time is that students should be taught through their mother tongue and after their progression to a certain stage, they should be given option to learn other languages of the world. Education should be given in mother tongue itself. I have also placed the opinions of Mahatma Gandhi, Vinoba Bhave and eminent linguists, besides studies made by organisations and individuals of the whole world in the context of languages.

—23 Dec, 2014

□

Eradicating the Venomous Vine of Anglicised Mentality

On 2nd April, 2010 in the convocation Ceremony of Bharatiya Institute of Forest Management, Bhopal, the then Union Minister of Forest and Environment, Shri Jairam Ramesh removed his ceremonial gown and headgear, and said that this symbolised British barbarism. He further asked as to why we were still wearing the symbol of British barbarism. This incident gave birth to a new debate in the country. On the reaction of Shri Ramesh, some educationists gave positive opinion. But this did not go down well with some educationists.

The Vice Chancellor of Delhi University, Prof. Dipak Paintal said that after Independence, most of the works in the country were being done on the pattern of the British. He believed that we were not copying any wrong thing. If we completely stop copying them, then we should discontinue English education and Ph.D. degree too. He further said that customary tie-coat-trousers were also not Bharatiya. The Vice Chancellor of Guru Govind Singh University, Prof. D.K. Bandopadhyay believed that this is no topic of debate at all. If the tradition is beneficial, what is wrong in continuing it? The university has to take a decision on this. In the Rabindra Bharati University of Kolkata, convocation ceremony is organised in ethnic attire.

The President of DUTA and Secretary of Jamia Milia Teachers' Association favoured retention of ceremonial gown. While batting in favour of gown, the Dean of Jamia Hamdard

University, Prof. Aftab Alam said it is worn in America also. He further said that the Bharatiya law is also based on English system, then what will be done of this? The Vice Chancellor of JNU, Shri B.B. Bhattacharya said that the use of colour gown in the convocation ceremony is heritage of the past. Jairam Ramesh had said that the universities linked to church were obliged to follow the culture of the church. If it is considered barbaric in Bharat then in Oxford, Cambridge, European and American universities, its use should be deemed uncivil. One gentleman went to the extent of asking that since Kurta-pyjama are a symbol of the slavery of the Mughal period, will he abandon this?

From the above comments, some important facts emerge. Some scholars said that since the tradition of gown and cap is good, it should be continued, but they did not explain why it is good. Is it a good tradition because it is a contribution of the British? The Vice Chancellor of JNU said that this is a heritage of the past. When the vice chancellors of prominent universities express such opinion, then it seems that Macaulay is really successful in achieving his aim, because they consider the tradition of merely 150 years as our past. Is our past so short, or our vision has become myopic? Today's world accepts that the *Rig Veda* is the oldest treatise of the world. Some years ago, some remains of 9000 year-old ancient civilisation were found in Khambhat of Gujarat. The whole world endorsed this finding. This is an example of what is called at present the international proof of a thing. As regards to Ramsetu, NASA itself has uploaded its photographs on its website. This is the historicity of our culture and traditions.

Prof. Aftab and the Vice chancellor of JNU said that the tradition of donning convocation gown is followed in Europe and America. If we consider it to be barbaric, then it would be considered uncivil there too. The opinion, that the traditions accepted in Europe and America should be accepted by us is simply ridiculous. Such a thinking of scholars evinces their willingness to blindly follow the west. Moreover, Europe and America have adopted Christianity and so, if practices prescribed by the church are followed there, it is quite natural. But Bharat has the avowed policy of equal respect for all religious. The gentleman who called Kurta-pyjama a Mughal attire, seems to have a superficial knowledge of history. The Vice Chancellor of Delhi University said that the formal dress of the corporate sector, coat-pant-tie, came from abroad. Well, if someone wears coat-pant in cold climate, it is okay. But at 45 degree celsius temperature in the summer season, if someone wears this dress, it will be considered sheer foolishness. If a dress has element of compulsion in it, or it has nudity and vulgarity, or it is incompatible with time and clime, or it is unscientific, how can it be approved?

Some gentlemen, while opining in the negative, indicated towards some relevant facts. Prof. Paintal said that if we were to discard western ceremonial dress, then we will also have to discard English and Ph.D. degree. Prof. Aftab, the Dean of Jamia Hamdard said that Bharat's law is also based on English pattern. These are not rooted in our country and are not compatible with our culture and ethos, then what hesitation do we have in changing them? This is not a mere hesitation but a feeling to avoid imminent hullabaloo by so-called secular scholars who react like this at any attempt to change anything as per Bharatiya angle. The stereotyped narrative of all their loud protest would be that secularism is in danger because everything is being saffronised. They will start shouting while branding us as old-fashioned and non-progressive.

Former HRD Minister, Dr. Murli Manohar Joshi and writer Amritlal rightly said that anything that is incompatible with our culture and ethos, should be changed. Dr. Joshi further said that the use of gown in convocation began when in western countries, education was controlled by church. The Chief Minister of Bihar, Shri Nitish Kumar rightly said that there should be a countrywide debate on this issue.

In fact, all sorts of arrangements or systems of the country should be compatible with our culture and ethos. To put it in other words, all systems should be scientific and logical. All the traditional systems of Bharat were adopted after deep and prolonged thinking. Therefore, it is necessary to reconsider all the systems began after the British came here upto the present times. The reconsideration should begin with education sector. Education is the base of all systems. There used to be foreign invasions for hundreds of years, aliens also ruled us, but our systems were not affected much until the British arrived and ruled us for 150 years, and made extensive changes to our traditional system. The well planned change by the British began with the introduction of Macaulay's model of education. In education sector, they first changed the medium of teaching and learning. Later, they changed the whole educational system. After Macaulay changed our educational system, he wrote to his father that he successfully did this, and he was happy, but his actual success would be in the continuity of this system even after they would have left this country. The people obtaining their education will look like Bharatiya, but in conduct, behaviour and thinking will be completely non-Bharatiya. This prophecy of Macaulay appears to have materialised. The British had to enslave Bharat, they had to wipe out its culture and traditions, in which they were successful to some extent. If we have to revivify our country, or we have to make our country prosperous and powerful, or we have to make it mentor of the world, we need to take a cue from the method of the British which proved efficacious in their way. In other words, we have to make radical change in education, and, first of all, to resurrect the lost glory of Bharatiya languages.

—31 March, 2010

□

Oppression of Women: Causes and Remedies

The incidence of gruesome rape on 16th December, 2013 shook the whole country. The youth agitated on the roads. On political level also, bitter debate going on. The lead issue of different news channels and newspapers continued to be this incident for a considerable period of time. But the other side of the scene is that the incidence of such heinous crimes is increasing and old cases are also surfacing.

After the incident of 16th December, the popular debate in the country centred on rape, oppression and similar issues. This is necessary too but when we gauge the present scenario, we find that oppression of women, violence against women and incidence of loot or robbery of women are fast increasing. Other issues are less in discussion. When an incident regarding other issues will occur, a heated debate on that will follow. This is our mindset in the context of social issues. This indicates a deterioration in the quality of social mind of the society, which is causing gradual decline in the health of the social system. It becomes imperative that we should think on this in totality and find out practical solution to the problem. The incident of 16th December was a result of deteriorated social condition. An effective permanent solution to any problem needs to be based on an analysis of its root causes.

Some amount of debate also centred on reformation of law, insufficient and inefficient policing and insensitive attitude of the police personnel. These need to be addressed and suitable improvement must be made. In the last year, there were 700 incidents of rape, out of which only in one case, the culprit could be prosecuted. This shows the massive shortcoming and inability of the present legal system. Even this data are also imperfect, because many incidents are not reported to the police. An incident was reported in a newspaper in which an auto rickshaw driver admitted that he had raped eight women so far, out of which only two filed formal complaint. Another fact of the legal system is that the case is heard in the court for years together, and the justice coming after a lapse of so many years loses its relevance. Suitable reformation in the legal system is required to curb this phenomenon. The number of fast-track courts should be increased and the victims of such cases should be delivered justice within a respectable period of time. In addition to this, the number of police personnel should be increased and they should be made more alert and efficient. Some more suitable measures can be taken to ensure quick disposal of justice, severe punishment and other related things. The fear of severe punishment can deter some persons from committing such crimes, but does it ensure complete solution of this problem? When we delve deep into the issue to analyse its roots, we find that the mother of the causes of such crimes is the insensible continuance of the legal and administrative system which the British put in place for their benefit. Police and administrative personnel behave with common man in the same indifferent way as it was customary in the colonial period. People find it difficult to meet officials of high ranks. Members of the political executive find it convenient and dignified to stay cosy in the security cover of police personnel keeping common man at bay. The police and administration treat common man more as their foes than friends. The Viceroy's residence before 1947 is now the President House. The parliament made by the British is now our Sansad Bhawan. Administrative system remains unchanged. Mostly the same laws are still in force. If we have to make our country Bharat instead of India, we should set up systems compatible with culture, ethos, traditions and our specific needs. Of all such systems, education is both pivotal and most important system. We need to begin with education.

In course of extensive debate on this issue going on in the country, one view frequently, and emphatically, emerged that we ought to bring change in attitude. This view merits consideration, but whether such a change can really be effected is a million dollar question. Can we bring about desired change by pronouncing capital punishment or strengthening police force or uploading the names and identity of rapists on the internet? In my view, a change in attitude is possible only through thoughts. The change in thought is possible through the *sanskar* of the family, inclusion of moral values in education and a *sanskar*-wise mature social ethos. Once I visited a prominent physician of Kanpur. In course of table talk, he said when we are in Mumbai, we form a queue for boarding a bus, but as soon as we reach Kanpur station, we forget this and begin indisciplined behaviour. The import of this example is that the behaviour of a person is accordant to the general atmosphere of the society he is in.

Any change in our attitude towards women will have to be begun from our family. Our behaviour with sister, daughter, wife, mother etc. in the family should be courteous and respectful. The family in which women do not enjoy a respectful status, that is not an equitable family. In some families, working women who earn for the family get higher honour than those only managing the household. This attitude needs to be changed. In the contemporary rat race of materialism, people do not pay required attention to children in the family. Parents have no time to spare for this. Parents of children from poor families keep struggling for a square meal, and they have no time for their children. In such a situation, proper development of children is not possible. If both mother and father work to meet their material needs, they have no time for children. Therefore, in affluent families mostly, their children are becoming victims of the wrong culture of drinking and dancing in clubs. In such families, children are entrusted to the care of maidservants or caretakers. In such a situation, from where will the children get parents' love, affection and desired *sanskar*? When a child does not get love and *sanskar* from his parents, he becomes an discontented and intolerant adolescent. The culture of openness and nudity prevalent in social life is further complicating the problem.

Most of the movies and television channels portray women as a material for enjoyment. All such things are available on computer and internet. In such a situation, greater wisdom and *sanskar* needs to be developed in children. The best way to do this is to deal with children in sensible way, to communicate with them on important issues and to keep them drenched in parents' love and affection. If suitable efforts are made on this line, the problem is possible to be solved. Once I called upon a friend of mine who worked in a television channel. The television set was kept in inverted position. I asked if it was out of order. He answered, "No, Atulji, my son is preparing for secondary board examination. So we decided that we will not watch television". I asked his daughter who studied in class IV as to why she was not watching television. She endorsed her father's explanation outright. This sort of sensibility can be developed in children even today. What is needed is a cautious and sensible behaviour of the parents. It is usually the case that when the child comes to watch television, he is rebuked and asked to go for his studies, and after the child leaves, rest of the family continues to watch television. This develops a negative reaction in that child's mind. Parents should keep this in consideration.

We are not mindful of one important issue. About 30-40 years back, children developed sexual instinct as well as its awareness at the age of 16-18, and at this age itself, they used to get married. But now, the age of development and awareness of their sexual instinct has dropped down to 10-12, while the average age of their marriage has scaled upto

30. How adolescents and youth should maintain restraint or abstinence, is a matter of great concern. Earlier, so much of openness and technology to display such contents was not available. Hence, in the present times, greater efforts and dialogue need to be made to inculcate proper *sanskar* and wisdom in them. A comprehensive discussion and debate on this subject in society has become imperative.

The most important reason behind imbalance between biological reality and moral obligations regulating its fulfilment lies in the faulty shape of education as a means of enlightenment of young learners. The danger of immorality to develop in the youth looms large over that country in education whereof values, morality and spirituality are not included. Maharishi Aurobindo said, "Since the time education of the country was detached from values, it lost its direction". In most of the families, there is a deficiency of *sanskar* because the parents of the present-day children are also the products of the same education. In my opinion education must yield at least three concrete benefits—(i) holistic development of personality and character, (ii) fulfilment of the needs of society and country, (iii) solution of national and international challenges. The present education hardly gives any such result. The bitter irony of this disturbing situation is that the Hindi textbook of NCERT has in its content, lessons which demean women. As an example, a dialogue from the book entitled *'Kritika'*, class IX, lesson title—'The Backbone', pp 35-37, author—Jagdish Chandra Mathur, is quoted below:

Prasad: Tax on beauty! (Ram Prasad and Shankar laugh). It is no joke, Saheb, it is such a tax gentleman that the tax-payer will never object to. However, the condition is that every woman should be left free to fix the amount of tax in proportion to the 'standard' of her beauty. Then see and behold, how the government income swells.

Prasad (interrupting): This is another matter, Babu Ramswaroop, I had told you earlier too, the girl being beautiful is highly necessary. Howsoever it is. Whether she has to apply cream and powder, or naturally. The issue is that, even if you and we agree otherwise, women of the house never agree.

Prasad: This is about education!.....yes, it is pretty clear Saheb, we need not keep a Mem Sahib in the house. Who will bear with her frivolities? She should be a matriculate at the most. It is okay, Shankar?

Shankar: Yes, yes. The question does not arise.

Ramswaroop: There is no question of job.

What an attitude will develop in students on reading such types of contents in textbook? Therefore, if we have to change the attitude of the society, we will have to rethink about the direction in which we have set out. A change in our direction will change our condition. In order to change the direction, we will have to change education after changing the country's systems.

If country is to be changed, education will have to be changed. Therefore, all the commissions constituted for education recommended value-based education, but it has not been included in the country's education until now. Wherever there was an attempt by social outfits at providing education combining values and morals, results were encouraging. Led by Shiksha Sanskriti Utthan Nyas, the education of personality development and character building was given in three schools. After the course was over, the students of three such schools were given examination without teachers as invigilators in the examination rooms. The results were positive. Such experiments may be extended to the whole country. What is required is the strong will of the central and state governments. The efforts like these cannot lead to finality by government's sole efforts. A positive role of society, especially people linked to education sector, is highly expected.

—2 Feb, 2013

□

Social Harmony: Experienced Live

This is an anecdote of 1980-81, when I worked in Akhil Bharatiya Vidyarthi Parishad (ABVP). We decided to start a Sanskar Kendra. We went to a small habitation in Jamnagar of Gujarat for expansion of our work. We went to a temple in that area along with a lady, who was an inhabitant of the place, to identify the spot where we could run a Sanskar Kendra. It was a good place for the purpose, and we also got permission to open our centre there. Then, we decided to sit at the lady's place for some discussion. She offered us some chairs outside her house and asked for some soda or lemon. We said that we were thirsty, so we would take water first. With surprise, she asked if we would really drink water of her house. When we answered in the affirmative, an atmosphere of deep delight spread in the household. Then we were served water, hot tea and breakfast. This strengthened the foundation of the Sanskar Kendra.

This is an anecdote of 1982-83, when I was a district convenor of ABVP. We chose a worker from Scheduled Caste community as a local *Vistarak*, for extension of organisational work. A *Vistarak* in ABVP works away from home, resides in its office and takes his daily meal with families of local workers. His meal was fixed in our house also once in a week. I informed my family about this. From the name of the *Vistarak*, my grandmother identified his caste. She reacted and asked me as to why I bring such people to be fed in our house. I explained to her that he is a *Vistarak* worker, who depends on the families of local workers for his food. My grandma advised me to feed him somewhere outside for which she would pay. Then I put my feet down and said that then I would also dine outside. The affection for her grandson finally made her agree to it silently. After this, that worker regularly visited our house and he would get his food even if I were not available in the house. Once, while dining together, we shared one plate. When he had gone away, my grandma chided me saying that feeding him in the house was okay, but why should I eat with him from the same plate? I just laughed without saying anything.

In 1986, I was on a visit (*pravas*) to Patan (university centre) of Gujarat. I called upon a new worker where I saw a senior person sitting on earth outside his house. I became curious to know why such a senior person sat like this. We had breakfast and tea inside the house. When that worker sat on sofa, his pet dog also sat by his side. When we came out, I found that senior person sipping tea from a saucer. I watched him clean the saucer with water poured into it by that worker, and put it at a place in the open, which was earmarked for piling such pots. What I watched made me seriously think about our mentality that allows an animal to sit and dine inside the house but excludes, as a rule, a senior person from this privilege on social consideration. I began to think as to when this situation would change and how society would be harmonious? This question still teases my mind.

In 1990-91, ABVP decided to observe Birth Centenary of Dr. Babasaheb Bhim Rao Ambedkar. My headquarters at that time was Vadodra and I was the secretary of the Birth Centenary Committee. I met a nationalist industrialist wishing to make him the President of this committee. No sooner had I mentioned Dr. Ambedkar's Birth Centenary that he showed strong reaction as to why we should celebrate the birth centenary of a person who had renounced Hinduism. I was pretty junior to him in age. Moreover, he was an eminent person from the points of view of experience, learning and social prestige. Still I placed my arguments with humility, although it is usually not proper to argue with such a senior person. I gave him some reading material on Dr. Ambedkar, and prayed to him that if he is convinced, he should accept our proposal. Eventually, he agreed to become President of the Birth Centenary Committee. This anecdote exemplifies how much illusion pervades the society regarding Dr. Ambedkar.

In 1991-92, I was in Karnavati (Ahmedabad). A government hostel for Scheduled Caste students was situated near our office. I developed some contact over there and became its frequent visitor. I came in contact with its warden. On 6th December of every year, ABVP celebrates Social Harmony Day. In consultation with the warden and some boarders of the hostel, we organised this programme in the hostel. When I started to speak in the function, three or four students began to protest saying that we had no right to speak on Dr. Ambedkar because we were his adversaries etc. When they came to peace, I asked them as to which books of Dr. Ambedkar they had read. They remained silent. I told them the names of books on Dr. Ambedkar and their authors and asked them if they had read them. I said further that since I had read those books, I had greater right on Dr. Ambedkar than them. They sat back on their seats, and the programme was conducted with elan. From this experience, it is naturally revealed that we have divided our great personages into social classes and dirty politicking is being done in their names. All the personages from Dr. Ambedkar to Sardar Patel belonged to the whole Bharat comprising myriads of social classes interwoven into one indivisible entity. I wish to develop this feeling in the general masses.

In 1993-94, on the pious day of Ramnavami, I invited twenty students of the Scheduled Caste hostel for dinner at the house of the City Mayor, prominent industrialists, Vice Chancellors, Principals of colleges etc. I personally accompanied a group of such students to the house of the Mayor. When students entered his house, he personally welcomed them and seated them in his guest room with due honour. All were introduced to one another. All of us sat on the dining table where the family dined everyday. The Mayor herself served food and helpings with care and affection. After dinner, we were again seated in the guest room where we were served ice-cream. And according to Gujarati tradition, all of us were served mouth-cleaning chewables. Finally, the students were seen off by the Mayor with gift of clothes.

There appears today an acute shortage of harmony in the required measure. Society is divided by narrow domestic walls of caste, language and region, touchability-untouchability, man-woman, rich-poor, city-village etc. Its root cause, to my mind, lies in the fact that we have deviated from our culture. Spiritualism is the only thing capable of converting Bharatiya culture into a nation. Spirituality means coming close to *atma* or elemental self, and realising its existence and potential. After getting close to *atma*, one realises that the same element or *atma* dwells in every individual which is a 'God particle'. When all of us consist of the same particle of God i.e. Supreme Soul, then why should there be any difference or discrimination in our collective existence? The closer the mass thinking gets to this eternal truth, the earlier will a solution of such social disharmony be at hand. Only after this, we can realise the coveted dream of making a harmonious Bharatiya society with one mind.

—25 May, 2016

□

Adolescence: Issues and Solutions

Adolescence is an important phase of human life when, in a way, the line and direction of man's life is set. If an adolescent gets proper guidance, he treads a right future path. But the contemporary state of social disharmony and materialistic dimensions of life, largely divorced from ethics and morality, are misguiding the adolescents in a dangerous way resulting in loot, burglary, drugs, alcohol, rape and violence becoming the way of their life. It's unmistakable purport is that we are not paying due attention to the negative issues they are naturally exposed to, to keep them on the right track without letting them divert and to set the right direction of their progression in all spheres. Adolescence is a sharp turn of human life that sets forth his future course. In the whole world, Bharat is considered a country of youth by virtue of massive population in the contextual age group. This specially necessitates a serious thinking on the issues of this age group and their resolution.

In our opinion, there are four aspects of the issues of adolescence which require our attention with all earnestness.

(a) **The Age Span of Adolescence in the Present Context:** Normally, the age group of 13-18 is deemed adolescence. In changed social conditions, however, the age group needs to be re-adjusted in view of the fact from social and biological angles that today's child is attaining adolescence earlier than it is officially specified. For re-adjustment of the age span of adolescence, it is imperative to consider the following two angles:

(i) **Social Angle:** In the present social conditions, a child of the present day fast becomes, mentally and temperamentally, a youth because the style of living and food habits have undergone a sea-change. Materialistic attitude further compounds the problems.

(ii) **Scientific Angle:** With changed food habits and social conditions, children are physically growing at a fast pace. Hence, it is necessary that while defining the age of adolescence, the aspects of physical and scientific changes of children must be properly considered.

In view of the facts enumerated above, the age span of adolescence may be defined as 12-16.

(b) **Specialities of Adolescence:** Adolescence has its own specialities of distinct nature which, if properly harnessed and guided in the right direction, can save from deviation. Adolescents have positive features in them which should be identified and given a right orientation. Some of these are as follows:

(i) They have a strong inquisitive tendency.
(ii) They have abundant energy.
(iii) They have a tendency to emulate.
(iv) They have plenty of information.
(v) They tend to be ideologists.
(vi) They have abundant creativity.
(vii) They have competitive attitude.
(viii) They tend to be gaudy, artificial and decorative besides having a tendency to show off.

Prominent negative tendencies in this age group are impetuousness, sense of insecurity, inclined to oppose and fight, reactionary mindset and indifference to society. Actually, adolescence is the intervening phase between childhood of the past and youth of future. At this stage, the subject faces a confusing mixture of the diminishing feelings of childhood and increasing feelings of youth. This curious mental state combined with changing physical conditions, brings negative tendencies to the fore. The adolescents also develop an arrogant attitude towards their parents exemplified by their queer rebuttal like this—If you know, I know as well. Contemporary youth has become stubbornly individualistic, refusing to extend beyond his own self. He centres strictly on 'me, my, mine and myself.'

(c) **Issues emerging from Prevailing Atmosphere and Physical change:** At the stage of adolescence, a child is affected by changes at two levels—physical and mental. These changes bring with them some problems for the adolescent, which need to be understood in the context of his position in family, school and society.

(i) **At the level of family:** For the last few years, the joint family system is receding fast. In nuclear family system, parents have little time for their children. As a result, children develop irritation, dissatisfaction and frustration. Parents make all resources handy for their children but do not give personal attention to them.

(ii) **At the level of School**: The prevalent educational system is itself generating problems for adolescents. These days students in schools, instead of developing their natural interest in study, are encouraged to simply memorise and learn their study material to obtain good marks in examination. Such a training makes the adolescent weak and deficient in higher competition, leading to their depression and frustration in future.

(iii) **At the Level of Society**: The widening network of mass communication is showing them, and exhorting them to do, what they do not require. The adolescents have a natural fondness for, and eargerness to, acquire and use all the materialistic resources widely popular in society. Adolescents are lured through catchy advertisements and misleading news or notifications. Normally, an adolescent takes recourse to wrong and unethical means to acquire such things.

(d) **Solution**: It is amply clear that if we try at the right time to bring adolescents on the right path, the direction of his life may change. Efforts in this regard need to be made at three levels:

(i) **At the Level of Family**: Family is the first alma mater of a child where he learns since his birth. Hence, family has to play a significant role in initial indoctrination of the child. At the level of the family, the following efforts are suggested:

- Adolescents should be encouraged to take active part in social and familial functions while shouldering some responsibilities.
- The option of joint family should be revived with an intention to developing a feeling and notion of togetherness of members of the family.
- The seniors of the family should exhibit self-discipline in their conduct and behaviour because adolescents have a strong tendency of emulating their elders.
- The elements of human and worldly values are stored in adolescent's inner self, which should be augmented.
- Nicety of interaction and communication within family should be increased.

- Adolescent's tendencies should be judged and the positive ones should be promoted.
- They should be encouraged to read inspiring literature.
- There should be an atmosphere of affection, of uninhibited communication in the family.
- Unjustified demands of children should not be granted.
- Parents should not burden children with their own ambition regarding them and should save them from any other unwelcome burden.
- The atmosphere of the family should abound in *sanskar*.
- Adolescents should be duly informed about the anatomy and physiology of human body.
- Adolescents should be drawn close to nature so that they could strike a bond and affinity with it.
- It is practically useful to keep tabs on the child's friends.
- The family should respect the youngsters, and take their opinion in important matters.
- Dining, offering prayers and watching television should be a collective exercise of the whole family.

Apart from these, adolescents should also be informed about physical and biological changes taking place in them, also about their effects and results. Children are sensitive to, and curious about, such changes happening in them. If they are not sensibly counselled in time, they may take the wrong path.

(ii) At the Level of School: Student's character is built in school, therefore school and its teachers have a greater role on this count. School should make the following efforts:

- To orient students towards subjects of their taste and aptitude.
- Teachers' mode of communication should be effective and appealing.
- Teachers should try to identify the tendencies of each student.
- Teaching methods should undergo qualitative change with an intention to develop positive tendencies in students. This should be included in the curriculum of teacher-education.
- Moral education should be imparted through the conduct and behaviour of teachers as well as through an ethical atmosphere prevailing on the campus.
- Students should be encouraged to avoid general tendency of envious comparison.
- A Counselling centre should be functional in all schools, where students get solution to personal, social and psychological problems, besides practical guidance regarding their career or vocation.
- The abundant energy available in young learners should be channelised towards creative activities, pursuit of hobbies of their taste, physical exercise and other areas as per their aptitude.
- Any subject needs to be explained to students in logical and scientific way, so that they are convinced beyond any doubt.
- Good quality books should be collected in the library.

(iii) At the Level of Society: The adolescent of

our times learns most of the wrong habits and cultivates unwanted tendencies induced by society and included by media. In a situation like this, the role of society and media becomes very important. An adobscent's mind is very sensitive and receptive. It instantly grasps the evils prevalent in society. In this back-drop, the following efforts are required at social level:

- In youngsters, a predilection for social harmony, co-operative and benevolence should be cultivated.
- Adolescents should be encouraged to develop social cordiality.

(iv) At the Level of Media and Mass Communication: Adolescents watch with interest the contents served on media and wish to copy them in their lives. Thus, media becomes a potent source of inspiration to adolescents. Hence, media should make the following efforts:

- Media should give right and factual information. They should never publicise the news which may provoke adolescents to indulge in violent acts.
- Enticing and alluring advertisements should not be shown in media and movies.
- Cheap and obscene methods of publicity should be banned forthwith.
- Media should popularise respect for country's symbols of pride and create general feeling among adolescents.
- Media should promote creativity among adolescents. Youths are considered the future of a country. If youths are given the right direction and their energy is channelised for positive work, the country will proceed on the

path of development, otherwise violence, loot, arson and civil disturbance will proliferate, which is adverse to humanity and a civilised country. We should endeavour to give right direction to adolescents at all levels so that the country marches ahead towards glory and well-being.

—16 Nov, 2015

□

Environmental Study and Research Centre

Environment is a word with broad meaning which includes the whole cosmos. The word *paryavaran* has two phonemes—*pari* means 'all around' and *avaran* means 'cover'. Our world and we are covered by sky, water, air, earth, fire (the sun), forest, tree, river, ocean and fauna. The integrated form of all these elements constitutes environment in which we take birth, lead a life, breathe, flourish and do all our activities. Hence, conservation and sustenance of environment is highly necessary for the entire society and ourselves.

In our times, environment is getting fast polluted leading to its deteriorating inbalance. Water and air are most polluted. Melting of glaciers, global warming, greenhouse effect and emission of poisonous gases have punctured the ozone layer and international conventions are being organised to explore the way out. But the ancient saints and sages, learned gurus, visionaries and seers, poets and bards etc. of Bharat were alert about the impending danger of environmental imbalance. The entire Vedic literature as well as folk literature abound in generous praise for all the components of environment like sky-air-water-earth, in view of their special significance and advantages for the world. Not only this, the Vedic hymns considered all the components of environment as gods and sung psalms eulogising them. When we interpret the Vedic hymns and psalms from scientific angle, we learn about many scientific hidden facts about environment.

It is worth mentioning that contemporary scientists are conducting research and investigation on physical aspect of environment, besides thinking about it academically. But even after physical environment is cleansed, but man's mind, sensibility and inner self (*atma*) are not cleansed and the fire of envy-hatred, deceit and treachery, sensuality and anger etc. continue to burn, establishment of peace in the world is beyond imagination. Therefore, ancient seers and thinkers had emphasised the cleansing of man's spiritual environment along with physical environment. This idea was expressed in Vedic mantras like—तन्मे मन: शिवसंकल्पमस्तु (i.e. my mind should be enriched with pious and exquisite pledges), धियो यो न: प्रचोदयात् (i.e. may He—who live inside the earth, the sky and the heaven—stimulate and illuminate our soul), चरित्रन्स्ते शुन्धामि (i.e. I purify your character), etc.

In the context of facts discussed above, study and research in the area of environment is required which should be based on the Vedas and other ancient Bharatiya treatises while co-ordinating with them the conclusions of modern environmentalists. The positive solutions for environmental cleaning, its conservation and enrichment should emerge from such a co-ordination of the ancient and the modern wisdom about it. To attain this ambitious aim, the establishment of an Environmental Study and Research Centre is both relevant and necessary.

Work Plan

- Identification and study of environment in our daily life and living.
- On the basis of material related to environment available in our ancient treatises, to work out a practical plan to meet the challenges of contemporary times.

Research Work

- To convene meetings, workshops, seminars and conferences from time to time.
- To produce and publish relevant literature.
- Elaborate and meticulous documentation.
- To bring all organisations working for environment on one platform and to strike co-ordination with them. To extend this further to international level.
- To work on local to national issues of environment towards their solution.
- To prepare curriculum and study material for all levels of teaching and to make efforts to implement in institutions, both private and government.

Preparations

- Identification of place or spot for the centre.
- Building of the apex unit of the centre.
- Arrangement and use of audio-visual apparatus.
- Identification of partners of the plan.

Human Resources

- Office in-charge and office assistant
- Hindi and English typist.
- To begin with, one research scholar.
- For guidance of environmental scientists, an academic council and a managing committee.

Academic Preparation

An exhaustive list of all environmental study and research centres.

- A panel of names and addresses of important scholars, scientists, professors and authors active in the field of environment.
- Collection of literature, manuscripts, journals and

magazines on environment.

- A complete bibliography of books and journals, national and international, in the field of environment.
- A compilation of important subjects and topics for research in future.

Subjects for Study and Research

- Primordial sources of environment in Vedic Codes (*samhita*)
- Elements of environment in Upanishadic literature.
- References to environment in the branches of the Vedas.
- Environment in Smriti and Dharmashastras.
- Environmental awareness in the Balmiki *Ramayana* and the *Mahabharat.*
- Environment in Sanskrit literature.
- References to trees and vines in the Vedas and Sanskrit literature.
- Flora and fauna along with auxiliaries of environment like small insects and pests and nature in general in ancient literature of Bharat.
- Contribution of forest, trees, mountains, rivers, ponds etc. in environment.
- Environment and ecology
- Vedic methods of environmental conservation and pollution control, viz. oblation (*yagya*), plantation, water conservation etc.
- Scientific analysis of five elements (*panchtatva*)—earth, water, fire, air, ether—in environmental context.
- Environmental awareness in the Puranas.
- Mental environment in Vedic and Sanskrit literatures.
- Environment and Hindi literature.
- Environment in Chemistry.

- Modern sciences and environment.
- Environment and architecture.
- Causes and remedies of environmental problems of contemporary world.
- Comparative study of individuals working for environmental protection at national and international levels.

—7 Oct, 2009

□

Student Movement: Question of Relevance

A cursory observation of country's history reveals that all the important movements, whether social or spiritual or political, had in them important role of students and youths. Let us look back into our past. Chanakya had led an agitation against Nand, a corrupt king. A large number of students registered their direct participation in this. In the modern period, Swami Vivekananda was successful in re-establishing Hindu way of life and culture in the whole world. Vivekananda was himself a youth, in whose campaign a young girl from abroad along with students and youths of the country participated in large number. A good number of those youths also became celibate *sanyasi* later. Many youths sacrificed their lives following revolutionary movement with Bhagat Singh, Chandrashekhar Azad, Madanlal Dhingra etc. and many other youths came along the non-violent movement of Gandhiji. After organising Azad Hind Fauz, Subhas Chandra Bose exhorted the youths—'You give me blood, I will give you Independence'. Thousands of youths joined Azad Hind Fauz to offer their blood for country's liberation. In a way, Azad Hind Fauz was an organisation of youths. When Dr. Keshav Baliram Hedgewar founded Rashtriya Swayamsevak Sangh in 1925, mostly students were its members. In due course, hundreds of students devoted their life to the mission of the nation, and this continues today also. For the first time in post—Independence

Bharat, in 1974, Nav Nirman Movement was launched in Gujarat against corrupt rule. In 1975, massive students' movement was organised for a long period against the imposition of autocratic rule in the country. Later, Shri Jayprakash Narayan assumed its leadership and it came to be known as JP Movement. By dint of this movement, democracy could be restored and those willing to establish autocracy were defeated. From all these movements of varying nature, one fact common to all that emerges is that the youths of the country rose above their self-interest and showed their strong commitment to do something for society and the country. All these movements had a positive impact on society and the country.

Since 1947, we are following democratic system. Democracy is meant governance by the people, of the people and for the people. By implication, it has to be a system for the welfare of the masses. But the government and its system is beset with its intrinsic defects that compels it to misuse and abuse powers to retain itself forever in power. To prevent this, peoples' awareness, peoples' orientation and peoples' movement become sine qua non for safeguarding democracy. In a way, agitation of people is the soul of democracy. Wherever there is democracy, its people need to be ready for agitation, lest democracy may degenerate into autocracy.

In our country, some wrong notions have developed of late in the mind of the people. Agitation has come to be limited to dharna (sit-in) with placards and rally with slogan shouting. But actually all activity that activates people's mind and agitates their thought towards any anomaly in democracy comes under the purview of agitation. During Emergency of 1975, many newspapers had agitated the minds of the people through articles in their columns. Swami Vivekananda enlivened people through his talks and speeches. Dr. Hedgewar inspired people by his way of life and conduct. Preparing a write-up on an issue and distributing it to a thousand people is also a component of agitation. Another aspect of agitation is that it should not focus on the interest of a person or a group, but on the general well-being of society and country. Students, who have little self-interest, are most capable of leading an agitation. As such, they have always been the backbone of all agitations. This is true for all countries. In 1960, there was a successful movement against Sukarno, the dictator of Indonesia. In 1990s, the corrupt ruler of Indonesia, Suharto, was unseated under pressure of student agitation. The educational movement of France in 1968 is also a relevant example. Such agitations happened in many countries of the world. Student agitation was relevant in the past, it is relevant in the present, and it will continue to be relevant in future. It is an eternal truth.

For the last few years, the society and the country as a whole especially administration, have developed a negative attitude towards student movement in general. This is unfortunate. In their view, student movement is analogous with arson, fracas and indiscipline etc. If it is seen in student movement, its reasons need to be identified. In most of the cases in which their agitation deviated to wrong path, the reasons are their misuse for mean political interests by political people. This is also true, but not proper or acceptable, that non-violent agitations carried out in ethical way fail to achieve their objective while violent agitations are placated with quick fulfilment of their demands. Who is responsible for this? Whether it is students or administration? It is the responsibility of all to ensure that the direction of student movement is not lost. Only students are not responsible for this. The other side of the scene is that teachers' organisations, workers' unions, employees' unions are recognised by the government but student organisations are not. In many democratic countries including America, student organisations are legally recognised, but why not in Bharat? It is sheer injustice with, and insult to, the student community of the country. All student organisations need to think collectively on this issue.

The general scenario of student agitation in Bharat is far from satisfactory. When we delve deep into its reasons, these facts surface. Since the wave of globalisation, liberalisation and privatisation started sweeping various sectors, especially economy, an atmosphere of cut-throat competition was created. Students also became its victim. Student has also become highly sensitive about his future and is endeavouring to earn the maximum he can. Secondly, politics has begun to influence all sectors of society in greater measure and as its natural fallout, students are strongly attracted to politics. The student movement of Assam in 1980 against infiltration of Bangladeshi citizens is an important instance of this. Majority of student organisations have been reduced to being political puppets leading the common students to lose faith in such organisations. Political parties are interested in keeping student organisations dependent on them. For these reasons, daring and combative youth leadership is hardly available in the country.

In this backdrop, some people have begun to feel that student movement is almost dead, and it is not possible to revive or resurrect it. This is negative thinking. But I sincerely believe that despite all such adversities, students can still agitate. At times, it does appear in immature form. For example, students actively participated in the movement for creation of a state of Telangana out of Andhra Pradesh. But the need of the hour is decisive student movement and struggle. Secondly, the scenario is pretty changed today, which we term 'Paradigm shift'. In current situation, it is nearly impossible to expect result from wayside agitation. Majority of students are nationalistic, but their situation and mindset prevent them from agitating on streets, but they are willing to participate in it, directly or indirectly, like those leading movement of thought on the social media. Internet is a medium through which global movement can be operated. The role of judiciary has also increased these days. The use of country's parliament, legislative assemblies, and their statutory committees can be helpful. Shiksha Bacho Andolan experimented with these modes while struggling for a mission, and we reaped decisive success. Usage of this means does not preclude the utility of rally, sit-in (*dharna*) and street protest. These are essential, but other supportive means are also fruitful. In other words, the need of the time is a proper combination of intellectual and combative leadership.

In this age of globalisation, the poor is getting poorer. Unemployment is increasing day-by-day. The evil of corruption is getting acceptance as a way of life. A situation is fast developing in which children of the rich alone will get higher and vocational education. In such a situation obtaining of late, student movement is direly needed. With this view, Swami Vivekananda said—उत्तिष्ठ जाग्रत प्राप्य वरान्निबोधत—i.e. arise, awake and stop not till the goal is reached.

—3 Nov, 2014

□

Sense of Duty of Teachers

ॐ असतो मा सद्गमय, तमसो मा ज्योतिर्गमय, मृत्योर्माऽमृतंगमय॥

—*वृहदारण्यक उपनिषद्*

"Ohm, lead us from unreality (of transitory existence) to the reality (of the eternal self), lead us from the darkness (of ignorance) to the light (of spiritual knowledge), lead us from the fear of Death to the knowledge of Immortality".

—*Vrihadaranyak Upanishad*

This is the aim of education. There should be no difference between the aim of life and education. Many great personages have expressed this opinion in different words.

"Perfection is inherent in man in a nascent state, an overt manifestation whereof is the aim of education".

—*Swami Vivekananda*

The teacher is a maker of man

—*John Adams*

मातृ देवो भव, पितृ देवो भव, आचार्य देवो भव (तैत्तिरीयोपनिषद्)

"Mother should be treated as a god, father should be treated as a god, teacher should be treated as a god."

—*Taitireeyopanishad*

In fact, teaching is not a profession but a mission for a teacher. In the life of Shri Prafulla Chandra Roy, this is practically exemplified, but the present scene is opposite to this. Presently, there is an acute crisis of both character and commitment. It is only through the character and commitment of teacher that student's character building and holistic development of personality can be possible. In this context, the following four types of commitment are imperative:

1. Commitment to the Student

Acharya Vinoba Bhave had said that we belong to the clan of teachers (*Acharya Kul*). One who teaches by his conduct, is a teacher. This tradition has been continuing in our country and its examples are available in every age and time. In the present times, however, the tradition has, more or less, weakened.

Once Hanumanji insulted an incompetent teacher. A complaint against him was put up before a senior teacher, who declared that as a penance for Hanumanji's misdemeanour, he would observe fast for the whole day. This act of the senior teacher had a deep impact on Hanumanji, who also observed a day's fast and did hard physical labour to atone for his fault. In the same way, such examples are visible in modern times in the life and conduct of ideal teachers like Shri Prafulla Chandra Roy and Prof. Yashwant Rao Kelkar.

Shri Prafulla Chandra Roy used to keep students from villages, who had housing problem, in his own residence. He would also pay fees of poor students. Prof. Yashwant Rao Kelkar never delivered long lectures, but brought positive changes in the conduct of his students through his own ideal conduct. When a student had no money to go and attend a conference, he gave him money. When that student began to earn, he came to Prof. Kelkar and wished to repay him. Prof. Kelkar put the money back in his pocket and advised him to use the money to help other students in need just as he had done for him. When I had to get admission in 11th, I had no money to pay the fees; a teacher of mine paid my fees. He used his salary in his entire life as teacher for the benefit of society.

There is an interesting story of a teacher who worked for students living in backward areas of Sweden. Once, irritated by the behaviour of his students, he commented, "You cannot do anything in your life and you will remain forever as you are now." At an interval of some years, he re-visited the same village. He found all his erstwhile students doing well in life. He surveyed the whole area with some of those students. He asked all of them the factors behind their success. All named one teacher who inspired them to become what they were. He became curious to know such a charismatic teacher. He met the teacher and asked him what did he do to push those students on the path of success. The teacher said that he did not do anything. The only thing he did was that he gave them love. From this experience, it comes to mind that honour cannot be demanded, it is earned.

Shri Guruji (the second Sarsanghachalak of Rashtriya Swayamsevak Sangh) was a professor in Kashi Hindu University. A student told him that since his preparation for examination was not complete, he would not take examination. Then Guruji offered to prepare him for examination. The student was from arts faculty, while Guruji taught in science faculty. But Guruji read his books of arts and prepared him for the examination. He passed the examination with good score.

Even in the awful educational system of today, if a teacher wills and wishes, he can make the subject appealing and can also inculcate in him awareness of values. He can give right direction to students. At a seminar in Surat, a lady teacher said that for the last twenty years, she would make her students chant the Gayatri Mantra at the beginning of every period. So far, no student had objected to this. She further said that she also made the students chant 'Ohm' three times before chanting the Gayatri Mantra. In some schools, this practice at the beginning of the period brought positive changes in students and infused discipline on the campus. Further, some practical elements may be included while teaching a subject.

Students can be taken on guided visits to observe the working in banks, offices and private firms, at least once in a week. In our traditional education system, there were thirty-two methods of teaching. We may not be familiar with all those methods, but at least teaching can be made interactive.

2. Commitment to the Subject

Ordinarily, knowledge doubles in five years. It is necessary that we (teachers) should also participate in, and contribute to, this. In the book entitled *'Treasure Within'*, published by UNESCO, it has been said—"Learning to learn, learning to do, learning to live together and learning to be". If a teacher begins to feel that he is only an educator, his own growth ceases. Hence, regular practice is compulsory. If Sachin Tendulkar would have thought regular practice was not necessary for him, he could not have become a great batsman of the world.

3. Commitment to the Society

A Bharatiya delegation was on a visit to America. At the conclusion of the visit, they met American President John Kennedy. They asked him as to how America progressed so fast. John Kennedy replied, "Every leader of ours, while teaching, thinks that all students before him are going to become the President of America in future". Kothari Commission said in its report that our university should not be like an island in the society, but a nucleus of social consciousness. In our school, college and university, a centre should be functional for developing social awareness and sensitivity as well as a strong *sanskar* of patriotism.

4. Commitment to Self

The *Kathopanishad* says—आत्मानं विद्धि—'recognise your own self'; Mahatma Budha said—आत्मदीपो भव—'be your own light'; Bhagwan Mahavir said—स्व में बस परसे खस—'focus on thyself, keep distance from others'. There is an interesting story in this context. A disciple of a saint was non-vegetarian.

He told him that when he listened to his talk, he would decide that he would not take non-vegetarian food in future. But that pledge did not translate into practice. What should he do? The saint advised him that he should try eating such food where no one could see him. The disciple thought that this could be feasible. When he longed to eat meat, he went to the outskirts of the village, where no one could see him. As soon as he was about to eat, he found that some animals were watching him. He climbed a hillock to eat, but there he found birds watching him. Finally he went inside the cave where none was watching him. But no sooner had he begun eating, a voice came from his inner self—'I am watching you'. The disciple completely abandoned non-vegetarian food. Do we look inside us, or at least towards us? Do we lead our life so superficially? Gandhiji gave an important call regarding life—'Plain living, high thinking'. A person living life on this principle, Chanakya, an *acharya*, developed a great ruler in Chandragupt.

Imparting education is a mission, not a trade. It is so because its pursuit is creation of man. Many *acharyas* like Chanakya, Prafulla Chandra Roy, Dr. Radhakrishnan, Prof. Yashwant Rao Kelkar etc. performed teaching duty with devotion. I humbly pray to God, 'He may give all of us the strength and devotion to tread the path paved by these luminary teachers'.

—11 April, 2014

□

Creation of New Alternatives of Education

Even after 73 years of Independence, we are stuck with dialogue and discussion only as to how our education should be. Many commissions and committees have been constituted post-Independence, which made good recommendations too. But these could not be implemented due to sheer lack of political will.

The Delors Commission of UNESCO reported that education of any country should be compatible with its unique nature and progression. Is our education today compatible with the nature and progression of our country? The answer is naturally in the negative. Education signifies an endeavour by which student's holistic personality is developed, and his character is built so that he fulfils the national and international needs, besides addressing contemporary challenges. Our fundamental concept of education is an eternal truth. On the basis of this, education should be value based, should be an amalgam of spiritualism and materialism, should be a sensible combination of the theoretical and the pragmatic, should be a fusion of present reality and futuristic vision, should be carried forth in the medium of student's mother tongue and it should be autonomous in system and structure. Drastic transformation of education in this direction is direly needed to be done in the whole country. The efforts being made by Shiksha Sanskriti Utthan Nyas are enumerated next.

In 2007, the central government proposed to introduce sex education. A countrywide agitation was launched against this. Many organisations joined this movement. As a consequence of this, the government had to withdraw its proposal. The union government and some state governments constituted committees to review the syllabus of sex education. When this movement was going on, our organisation submitted a petition to the Petitions Committee of the Rajya Sabha. The Committee admitted our petition for hearing and public hearings were organised in seven metros in which more than 40 thousand representations were received. Most of these representations were against sex education. The Petitions Committee kept working on these for one year and a half, before it prepared its report. The report was also signed by the Vice President of Bharat, and it was tabled in the Rajya Sabha. The Petitions Committtee comprising members of different political hues made the unanimous recommendation that instead of giving sex education, students should be given education of 'character building and personality development'. Shiksha Sanskriti Utthan Nyas also thought of proposing an alternative of sex education. Accordingly, we organised a national seminar on the subject at Pune on 21st and 22nd February, 2009. In this seminar, scholars from the whole country unanimously prepared a draft of syllabus and constituted a Syllabus Committee. This committee prepared a syllabus for 'Character Building and Personality Development' after its four-month toil. This syllabus was discussed in seven dialogue sessions organised across the country.

In all the seminars and dialogue sessions, students, teachers, parents, educationists and representatives of educational institutions numbering more than 1,200 participated. All the participants were expected to come with their suggestions after having read the whole syllabus. To consider the suggestions gathered in all the seven seminars, the Syllabus Committee sat together. After the conclusion of this chain of brain-storming sessions, the final syllabus was prepared which was entitled—*Vidyalaya Gatividhiyon ka Alay*—or school, the abode of activities. This syllabus is meant for teachers. For students, a separate programme has been chalked out on this basis. This programme is to be included in the current academics effective in school without introducing specific book or period of study for the subject. In order to practically implement this initially in 50 schools, a workshop of the principals of those schools was organised. In days to come, we wish to extend this activity to many more schools. The other side of it is that the Governments of Punjab, Himachal Pradesh, Chhattisgarh and Madhya Pradesh have decided to impart yoga education in place of sex education. The Government of Uttar Pradesh announced introduction of health education instead of sex education. Yoga and health have become the subjects of new curriculum.

In coming days, we plan to work on five different subjects like:

1. Value-based education
2. Vedic Mathematics
3. Environmental Education
4. Education through mother tongue
5. Autonomy of education

The details of work underway regarding these subjects are given hereunder.

1. Value-Based Education

All the commissions and committees the government formed after Independence, advocated value-based education. But until now, values have not been included in education. On the other side of it, there is near unanimity in society on this subject. In some private institutions values are being taught under various nomenclatures like religious education, moral and spiritual education, life skill, human values, life values etc. These titles may sound different but their subject matter does not vary much. It is necessary to bring all such institutions on a common platform. With this purpose, seminars were organised in Haridwar, Ahmedabad and Gwalior. Preparation of a comprehensive syllabus for this subject is required. For school level teaching, we have prepared syllabus for 'Character Building and Holistic Development of Personality'. In near future, we plan to convene a meeting at the national level to discuss modalities to include values in higher education. The work on future plan of action will follow this.

2. Environmental Education

What we call 'global warming' today has its concrete solution in our traditional stream of thought. Environment is mentioned in all our ancient religious treatises. Under a judicial order of the Supreme Court of the country, environment has been included in the curriculum for school level teaching. But this inclusion is haphazard, and lacks proper planning, suitable arrangement of teaching and, above all, a right syllabus. To bridge this gap, it is necessary that a syllabus is prepared on the basis of Bharatiya thoughts. To contemplate on this, a national level meeting was organised on 28th & 29th August, 2010 at Delhi.

3. Vedic Mathematics

On Vedic Mathematics, we began our work since last August. A council of scholars was constituted and four meetings of it have been convened. As a conclusion of deliberations in these meetings, it was resolved to organise five seminars in joint collaboration with different educational institutions. But the actual seminars held were six in number, in which 893 persons from 20 states participated.

Our future plan includes founding a 'Vedic Mathematics Research Centre' at Bhopal. Through this centre, we propose to do the following work:

- Preparing comprehensive syllabus for classes I to XII.
- Inclusion of Vedic Mathematics in higher education.
- Computer and Vedic Mathematics.

- Usage of Vedic Mathematics in competitive examinations.

The next year, we plan to organise national seminars on all the four subjects. Seminars and workshops are being organised at state level also.

4. Education Through Mother Tongue

There is hardly any country in the world, except Bharat, where primary education is given through foreign language. All the logic and scientific justification for choosing a language as medium of teaching unequivocally uphold mother tongue. The English left Bharat but people stay anglicised, so much so that from common man to learned scholars nurtured an illusion—which they firmly believe to be a reality—that any development of Bharat and its people is not possible without English. In the given scenario, the fight for language will have to be fought on a large scale. We will have to make much more efforts for reviving the lost status of our languages than what we have to do for changing the texture of education. We are making required contacts to advance our endeavour on this subject. Some efforts have also been initiated to encourage people to use one's own language in daily life. Some of these are as follows:

1. Putting one's signature in one's own language.
2. Whether speaking or writing in any language, even in English if necessary, using the word Bharat, instead of India.
3. All the programmes should be conducted in our own language.
4. The book entitled *'मातृ भाषा में प्राथमिक शिक्षा' (Primary Education in Mother Tongue)* has been distributed to 5,50,000 people. This book is planned to be published in different Bharatiya languages.
5. In order to promote work on this issue, a team of workers is being formed at the national level. Its meeting will be convened very soon.

5. Autonomy of Education

An autonomous educational organisation should be set up at the national level. This should be completely autonomous on the pattern of the Election Commission and the Judiciary. All the arrangements for the Election Commission and the Judiciary are done by the government but they do not hesitate in passing orders against the government. We believe that education deserves greater autonomy than these organisations. The Autonomous Educational Organisation should have its branches at state and district levels. Its draft has been prepared and a country wide discussion on it has been initiated. Further, efforts are direly needed to put in place a new educational order emerging from amalgamation of eternally valid principles and modern elements regarding every subject of teaching and learning. Out of this, a new alternative of education will naturally emerge.

—1 July, 2019

□

Kumbh: Inspiring Symbol of Bharatiya Culture

The Simhastha Mahakumbh, organised every twelve years was held at Ujjain, the city of Mahakal, from 22nd April to 21st May, 2016. This festival of Kumbh is very important in Hindu way of life in which crores of devotees take holy dip at the festival point of Haridwar or Prayag or Ujjain or Nasik. At each of these places, the Kumbh is organised every twelfth year in rotation. At Haridwar and Prayag, the half-Kumbh is organised in the intervening sixth year between two twelve-yearly Kumbhs.

As per astronomical calculations, this fair begins on the day of Makar Sankranti, when the Sun and the Moon enter the Scorpio Zodiac sign and Jupiter, the Aries Zodiac sign. This specific astronomical combination happening on the day of the Makar Sankranti is considered highly auspicious. It is believed that on such a day, the doors of heavenly domain open and the soul of the person taking the holy dip on the day gets easy entry to the heavenly domain. Taking a holy dip here is considered a virtual glimpse of the heaven.

Stories from the Purana

A few stories from the Purana, related to the Kumbh are popular. The most acclaimed of these is the story relating to the dripping of the drops of the nectar emerging from the churning of the ocean. According to this tale, when Indra and other deities were rendered weak by the curse of Saint Durvasa, the demons invaded and defeated them. Then all the deities collectively called upon Lord Vishnu and narrated the whole incident to him. Lord Vishnu advised them to extract the nectar by churning the ocean (क्षीर सागर) together with the demons. Accordingly, they entered into an alliance with the demons and set on churning the ocean. As soon as the nectar came out, Jayant, the son of Indra, fled into space with the pot of nectar. Next, on the order of Shukracharya, the mentor of the demons, the demons followed Jayant to retrieve the nectar. He was captured midway. Following this, a twelve-day incessant war was waged between the demons and deities.

While the war went on, drops of nectar dripped at four places—Prayag, Haridwar, Ujjain and Nasik. During this period, the Moon protected the pot of nectar from parturition, the Sun from breaking it, the Guru from its pilferage and the Saturn protected it under fear of Indra. In order to bring about truce, God assumed the face of a seductress (मोहिनी) and, as per His right, fed all with nectar in divided quantity. Thus the war of deity and demon was brought to an end.

The time at which the Moon and others ensured the security of the pot of nectar, the Moon and the Sun conjoin as ruling planets of the Zodiac sign of the time, the yoga of Kumbh is made. In other words, the year in which the planets Sun, Moon and Jupiter conjoin in a specific Zodiac Sign, the Kumbh is organised at the four places where the drop of nectar had dripped.

The antiquity of the Kumbh has not yet been measured with decisiveness. Who commenced it first, cannot be named with certainty. Whatever information about Amrit Kumbh Yoga are given in ancient treatises, have been described here. In all probability, the Kumbh Fair is as ancient as the Arya race itself.

The history of the public life of Bharat is known from the *Mahabharat*, the Bhagvat and the Puranas, and we are given to believe that such congregations have been traditionally held in Bharat since time immemorial. Innumerable saints and sages gathered in holy places like Naimisharanya, Kurukshetra, Prabhas etc. to perform yoga, *yagya*, spiritual medtation and spiritual dialogue. They also nourished and conserved dharma while pondering on the condition of the country and society, their nature and customs. In the Age of the Buddha, we see that Bauddha hermits popularised Sangh, Dhamma and preachings of Lord Buddha through huge conventions (संघ महासंगीति) at holy places from time to time. They also constantly contemplated on the ways and means for eternal welfare of the humanity. Bauddha King Harshavardhan used to organise Sarva Tyag Yagya (सर्व त्याग यज्ञ) at an interval of five years, where countless saints and sages assembled. This recalls the memory of the Kumbh Fair.

Acharya Shankar: The Organiser of Kumbh Fair

When malpractice, misconduct and debauchery started spreading fast in the country, Shankaracharya, a corporal embodiment of Vedic spiritualism, preached and popularised Vedanta in the whole country by virtue of his unparalleled brilliance and spiritual accomplishment. He founded four monasteries in the north, south, east and west of the country and launched spiritual consortium of ascetics and hermits. He also facilitated their presence and participation in the celebration of the astronomically conjoined phenomenon of Kumbh Yoga at the four mentioned places. He did this to conserve and popularise Sanatan Dharma. It is believed that the tradition of Kumbh fair commenced from this and it earned distinction in due course. Later on, all the sects and cults of the Sanatan Dharma began to partake of it, conferring the Kumbh fair with supreme glory and mass acceptability, leading to its colossus form in the present time.

In the Shrimad Bhagvat Gita, it has been said—तीर्थि कुर्वन्ति तीर्थानि—i.e., 'devotees like you, who carry Godhead within your heart, convert a place into a holy place of pilgrimage by your footfall'. In plain words, the place where saints and hermits assemble in lakhs, the land and sky, water and air, and even dust particles acquire holiness potent of giving salvation and become carriers of the fluid flow of religious feeling. The assembly of saints is the inner strength of Kumbh Common people visit the Kumbh more for a sight, touch and blessings of these saints than for sheer pilgrimage. The place where thousands of celibates and hermits assemble in search of eternity after conquering death, is duly potent to produce nectar. Kumbh Fair is like a spiritual rain showering nectar all around. The mysterious metaphor of the story from the Purana has assumed a physical shape in this form.

The festivals, fairs and ceremonies of Bharat have as much social and national value as they have spiritual value. All such activities have a pre-defined purpose and objective. Kumbh Fair too has as much social and national significance, as it has spiritual reverence.

Our sages and hermits were devoted to religious and spiritual contemplation in secluded mountain retreats, renouncing familial and social life. It is seen even today. The fairs like this also facilitate their get-together. Moreover, common people forgetting all artificial divisions of caste, language, province, sex etc. stay at one place in one large group. They reap the benefit of holy dip and inspiring vision of saints and sages. Crores of people from the country and abroad participate in this. In no other country of the world, such a spectacle is seen.

As of now, many perversities have crept in our society and country. Caste, language bias, untouchability, class distinction, the poor vs. the rich, man vs. woman, backward-forward divide, provincialism, communalism etc., are the malaise that plague our society but people rise above these cleavages to participate in the Kumbh with common notion, common devotion and common dedication. This is the real nature of the soul of the people of Bharat, but the pollution we see in the society is only its outer cover, which naturally and effortlessly vanishes in such holy celebrations exhibiting a cohesive Bharatiya society. The Simhasth Kumbh mega-fair presents to us an opportunity to watch our society sticking to, and moving towards, its roots. It also gives the participants an opportunity to move towards a pious life.

Inspired from the facts regarding the Kumbh Fair, the Government of Madhya Pradesh and some scholars working in social sector organised four international seminars, with participation of hundreds of scholars of the world, to orient the Simhasth Kumbh of 2016 towards its original glory and significance. The valediction of this churning of thought was performed on 14th May, 2016, in the final convention of the series. In the last convention, a conclusion of earlier four ones was presented, and adopted as a pledge. This pledge contained a guidance and direction for the people of Bharat and the world to achieve a peaceful and blessed life while co-existing with harmony.

Historic Celebration

Among the centres of ancient Bharatiya culture, Ujjaiyini has a special status. According to the *Mahabharata* and the Puranas, this city existed before these treatises were produced. Archaelogical excavations confirm the city to be approximately 3000 years old. Such an ancient city remained static despite historical upheavals and changes in its name. Of the many names of the city, Avanti and Ujjaiyini have been the most used ones.

The Kumbh Fair organised in Ujjain is termed as Simhasth. According to scholars, Simhasth Kumbh was also considered a conceptual congregation in the past. In the Simhasth Kumbh, saints and scholars from across the world contemplated on core issues of human life and living, and guided the humanity for leading a blissful life with peace and mutual cohesion.

To the common man and scholars of Bharat, such spiritual mega fairs appear natural because they are aware that in our country, these are normal practices observed perennially since ages. But for the whole world, this is an extraordinarily surprising event. Therefore, in every Kumbh, scholars from across the world participate at will to do research on the subject. Such scholars who visited the Kumbh of Prayag in 2013, observed that it was a unique and wonderful event since its management was so meticulous that no accident occurred there, and also because everything was planned and excecuted jointly by the administration and society. The Simhasth Kumbh of 2016 proved a source of inspiration for the country and the world. Come, let us be participant of this rich cultural tradition of Bharat.

—14 April, 2016

□

Srinivasa Ramanujan: An Inspiring Mathematician

Srinivasa Ramanujan is still shining like the Polar Star in the horizon of mathematics. He lived a short life of 32 years, 4 months and 4 days. The work he did in the short span of his life still baffle the mathematicians of the world after 100 years of his demise. They are still struggling to solve his intricate formulas.

Ramanujan began research work at the age of 13 and started documentation of his work since he attained the age of 15. It will not be an exaggeration to say that he was born with mathematics, devoted his whole life to mathematics and kept working until he was confined to deathbed. He was actually ill in London when Prof. Hardy called upon him. While he was on his way to Ramanujan's house, he decided not to discuss mathematics with him on that day in view of his ill health. It would be proper, he thought, to do some casual talk only. When he met Ramanujan, he told him that the taxi in which he came, bore the number 1729, which was an inauspicious number. Ramanujan shot back that it was not so, and explained that it was a very small number which can be represented in two ways as the cubes of two numbers added together. He exemplified his proposition as $10^3 + 9^3$ or $12^3 + 1^3 = 1729$. The famous mathematician rightly said Ramanujan was a friend of every number.

After returning to the homeland, Ramanujan's quest of

mathematics continued despite his incurable disease. In the words of his wife, Janaki Devi, "Lying on bed all the time caused ache in his legs and his whole body, but ignoring this, he would ask her to seat him on bed with support of pillows and in that position, he would get absorbed in mathematical calculations with slate and chalk. In his last letter written to Prof. Hardy on 12th January, 1920, just two months before his death, he had sent his findings on 'Mock Theta Function'.

Ramanujan was born in Erode, Tamil Nadu, in his maternal uncle's house on 22nd December, 1887. His father, Srinivasa Ayangar, worked as an accountant in a cloth shop in the village named Kumbhakonam in the district of Tanjavur. The economic condition of his family was just ordinary. His mother, Komaltammal, was a traditional lady of religious bent of mind.

With religious *sanskar* imbibed in his family, Ramanujan followed traditional religious way of life and offered worship every morning, always wore dhoti, and maintained head-tail. When Prof. Hardy invited him to come over to England, his mother said no to it because those days travelling across the sea was considered inauspicious. She feared that his son may have to take wine and meat abroad, which will pollute his *sanskar*. She was deeply devoted to the family deity Namgiri. One morning, she said that her deity had visited her in dream and she saw Ramanujan sitting with some respected Englishmen. She added that her diety had commanded her not to go against her son's wishes. Before setting off, Ramanujan promised his mother that he would strictly follow Bharatiya religious tradition and would stick to vegetarian food. On 17th March, 1914 he set out for England.

Ramanujan was brilliant as a student. In his school days, he received many awards and scholarships. In his examination of class XI, he failed in all subjects except mathematics. But his teachers were simply astonished to see the extraordinary quality of his answers in mathematics. At the age of 16, he had solved the equations and formulas of geometry and algebra in famous mathematician G.S. Carr's book. In 1902, he discovered some methods to solve cubic and biquadratic equations. In his school, there were 1200 students. The large number of students made it difficult to prepare the timetable of teaching. But Ramanujan was so adept in calculation that he did this work easily, and handed over the time-table to his senior, Subbiyar.

Having failed in class XI, Ramanujan started giving tuition to meet the needs of his family. After his marriage, he loitered to places in search of a job. During these six difficult years, his work on mathematics was hampered but some good souls like Deputy Collector Ramaswami Aiyyar, Prof. P.V. Sheshu Aiyyar, C.V. Rajagopalachari, Ramchandra Rao etc. helped him to work on a job while pursuing his mathematics.

In the life of Ramanujan, the most important role was of Prof. Godfrey Harold Hardy of Cambridge University, UK. When he saw his mathematical findings and research, he was simply astonished. In consultation with, and request to other mathematians of Britain, British officials in Bharat and administrators of the University of Madras, he called Ramanujan to England. He facilitated Ramanujan's entry into Trinity College of Cambridge as Fellow, had Scholarship granted to him and guided his study and research. He played the pioneering role in making him, who had failed in class XI, a great mathematician of the world.

Ramanujan lived in England from 1914 to 1919. During this period, he faced many ups and downs in his life. Despite obstruction in his research due to the First World War, difficulty in fooding for being a vegetarian and illness owing to excessive cold, he produced 37 research papers. On 19th March, 1916 he was awarded graduate degree by the University of Cambridge: On 6th December, 1917 he was made 'Fellow of London Mathematical Society' and in February 1918, he was made a member of the University of Cambridge. In May 1918, he got the honour of being the first Bharatiya to become a 'Fellow of Royal Society'. On 13th October, 1918 he was chosen to be the Fellow of Trinity College. These achievements must have made him proud of himself because his mentor, Prof. Hardy, also chaired this position in Trinity College, Cambridge.

Srinivasa Ramanujan tirelessly worked with mathematics and reached the pinnacle of academic accomplishment in his short life of 32 years. The research works done by him were applied to particle physics, computer science, cryptography, polymer chemistry, nuclear furnace, telecommunication, communication network, nuclear physics, medical science etc. Three of his manuscripts were published posthumously by Tata Institute of Fundamental Sciences. The work done by him in his last days recorded in 140 handwritten pages were retrieved by Prof. George Andrew, Visiting Professor of the University of Wisconcin of USA, from a book in the library of Trinity College. Prof. Andrews published this under a beautiful title, *'The Lost Notebook of Ramanujan',* on which mathaticians of the world are working. Recently, a mathematician of USA has claimed to have solved a formula sent to him in his last letter to him. There is an interesting story of 1921. A renowed Hungarian mathematician, George Polya, took one of Ramanujun's notebook from Prof. Hardy, to work on it. But very soon, he returned it to Prof. Hardy, saying that if he let himself be entrapped in the phantasmagoria of solving his formulas, it would consume his whole life, and he would not be free to do any personal research.

Renowned scientist and philosopher, Bertrand Russel said, "Prof. Hardy and Prof. Littlewood found out another Newton in a Hindu clerk". Dr. A.P.J. Abdul Kalam said, "Ramanujan continues to be a source of inspiration not for Bharat alone, but of the entire world". Prof. Hardy said, "He enriched my life, I cannot forget him". Prof. Hardy prepared a ranking of contemporary mathematicians on a scale of 100 points, in which he awarded 25 points to himself, to Littlewood 30, to German mathematician David Hilbert 80, and to Ramanujan he awarded 100 points.

In his five-year stay in England and for his work during this period, Ramanujan received a lot of honour and a number of awards, but he meticulously retained his original simplicity and distinctive Bharatiya way of life. Prof. Anandrao Ramanujan, his contemporary working in Kings College, opined that despite all name and fame, Ramanujan was humble by nature and simple in living. In England, he cooked for himself. He used to say, "If a mathematical equation or formula does not fill me with divine thought, my whole exercise is meaningless". When he was economically weak and he had no money to buy paper, he would write his new formulas on used pieces of paper in red ink. When he was in a job, he would collect waste paper around the Port Trust to write on. When he was awarded a scholarship of ₹ 250 by the University of Madras, he wrote to the Registrar of the University that out of this amount, whatever remains after supporting his family, should be deposited in the Poor Student Fund of the University.

The Government of Bharat declared the year 2011-12 as 'National Mathematics Year' to commemorate 125 years of Srinivasa Ramanujan's birth. 'Mathematics Day' is observed in the whole world on 22nd December, but it is unfortunate that in Bharat, sufficient research is not being done on the work of Srinivasa Ramanujan. The governments of the centre and states should plan to promote research on Ramanujan's work by inspiring and encouraging Bharatiya scholars of Mathematics.

The life and work of Srinivasa Ramanujan is a source of inspiration for students, teachers and mathematicians of India and the world.

—21 Feb, 2013

□

Educational Thoughts of Pt. Madan Mohan Malaviya

Mahamana was a highly revered and celebrated educationist of Bharatvarsha. He considered education as the greatest strength. He also considered illiteracy and lack of education as reasons of our subjugation. He also treated literacy and proper education as the only remedy for the country's plight. Malaviyaji firmly believed in what he said, "If you want advancement of your country, make every effort to ensure that no boy or girl of the country remains illiterate".

Mahamana considered education as a means of all-round development of human life. He opined, "That is real education which develops and enriches student's physical, mental and emotional faculties". He wished to develop education as a force to arouse patriotism so that the new generation could serve the society and the country selflessly. He wished to see a system of education develop in the country in which teaching and learning in primary and secondary schools were free. He believed, "At every stage, the financial management of education should be such that any child is not deprived of access to education on account of his poverty".

Pt. Mahamana Malaviya considered women's education more important than men's. He felt thus because woman bears and mothers the future generation of the country. He also wished that women of the country should be educated, under specific national programmes, in a way that they imbibe the superior aspects of the ancient and the modern knowledge in appropriate balance. He wished to strengthen and empower women to enable them to play substantial role in the reconstruction of the country.

Objectives of Education

Mahamana viewed in education a power capable of developing man, society and nation. With this perspective, he determined broad objectives of education:

1. **Holistic Developemnt of Personality:** Malaviyaji wanted holistic development of personality through education. Sheer intellectual development, he believed, is meaningless. He regarded a co-ordinated development of physical, mental, intellectual and emotional aspects of students as the sublime end of education.
2. **Physical Development:** Mahamana believed that a physically weak person cannot be expected to construct a strong nation. In one of his essays entitled, *"Mera Bachpan"* he wrote, "Health rests on three pillars—food, sleep and continence. Sensible management of the three will ensure sound health". He also believed that it is continence that endows a person with will-power and general strength.
3. **Education for Character Building:** Mahamana felt that character building is one of the objectives of education. Knowledge without modesty, in his view, is meaningless. He considered immaculate character more important than intellectual and commercial development for paramount growth of the individual and the nation.
4. **Development of the Feeling of Patriotism:** Malaviyaji considered development of the feeling of patriotism as an important objective of education. An educated person should exhibit selfless devotion to the nation. He said, "This Bharat is our country. No other country

of the world is parallel to it from all angles. We should be grateful to God, and take pride in ourselves, for being born in this country".

5. **Development of Feeling of Service:** Mahamana considered service as the greatest religious act. He perceived God's particle in every creature. He felt that service of the deprived, the exploited and the miserable people is the most appropriate means to realise God. He wanted to inculcate the feeling of service and habit of right conduct in the student from the very beginning.

Structure of Curriculum

Mahamana favoured a curriculum framed on a broad design combining the traditional and the scientific. He believed that it is not a static thing that remains the same at all places and times. It is dynamic in nature, which changes itself according to the needs of time and place. Mahamana advocated sensible inclusion of spirituality because this is the basis of character building. He also desired a blending of the ancient and the modern. The curriculum, he believed, should be an even mixture of science, fine arts and philosophy, besides other branches of knowledge.

Mahamana desired to see in teachers a high level of character, so that their students could emulate them to develop their own character. This is the greater purpose of education. As such, he expected from both teachers and students, high character and noble conduct

Duties of Students Identified by Mahamana

- They should first improve health, strengthen body, through physical exercise, and study thereafter.
- They should take plain and pure food regularly.
- They should include study in daily routine.
- They should value the sanctity of time.
- They should infuse spirituality in living.

Duties of Teacher Identified by Mahamana

- They should follow religion and religious treatises.
- They should exhibit good conduct.
- They should be devoted to the service of nation.
- They should make every effort for all-round development of students.

Pt. Mahamana Malaviya founded Kashi Hindu Vishwavidyalaya to walk his talk regarding education. This university is considered a premier university of the country even today.

—22 Oct, 2018

□

Educational Thoughts of Sister Nivedita

Sister Nivedita applied the educational principles of Swami Vivekananda in her school in Bharat. According to her, "We should be workaholic, energetic and dedicated to the service of humanity. Development of a steadfast, active and dynamic personality should be the goal of education". She distinctly believed that a true monastic person cannot be indolent or indifferent to the welfare of humanity. Moreover, he can neither hate someone nor ignore someone. Sister Nivedita's educational thought is based on monotheistic philosophy.

According to her, the aim of education is not only earning a livelihood, but it should be character building, personality development and national reconstruction.

- Education means a formal system that regulates wishes and converts them into action.
- So much contribution of ours is expected in educating a child as much we can aid the growth of a sapling.
- "If we do not 'sanskarise' or refine our feelings, we are not educated. Education without this means that we have learnt some intellectual craftsmanship, by displaying which we can earn our livelihood. But an education like this cannot arouse human feelings. This makes it pretty clear that we cannot become a human being just by virtue of intellectual accomplishment, but remain an active but fickle ape".

(The Complete Works of Sister Nivedita, IV, 1968)

- According to Sister Nivedita, "Value-based education is conductive to self-realisation by the learner. Such an education, by arousing our feelings, helps us experience the 'eternal truth' in the destitutes, the oppressed and the suppressed people and the class of daily-wage labour".
- Sister Nivedita opposed the foreign education system. She believed that education directly impacts society and its vice versa is also true. Hence our education system should include cultural traditions of Bharat, social values, social ideals and the aims of society. Her philosophy of education was inspired by the fact that education should inculate in students love for their motherland.
- Sister Nivedita did not consider sheer reading and writing as education, but gave greater importance to knowledge derived from experience. She writes, "The woman who understands the history of nation, who has visited some important places of pilgrimage and who has a clear conception of the nature of her country, is more educated than those who only read a lot and obtain only bookish knowledge."

(*Lectures & Writings of Sister Nivedita, 1975*)

Viewed in totality, the educational concept of Sister Nivedita is based on the twin principles of equity and diversity. An ardent advocate of women's education, Sister Nivedita favours a variegated curriculum incorporating spiritualism, technical education and higher research.

—24 Nov, 2018

□

Rashtrakavi Ramdhari Singh 'Dinkar': Herald of Bharatiya Nationalism

Rashtrakavi Ramdhari Singh Dinkar was a litterateur who promoted vigour, nationalism and Bharatiya culture. In true sense, the title of 'Rashtrakavi' is bestowed on only those whose literature abounds in the voice of nationalism in totality. The literature of the 'Rashtrakavi' is the cultural paradigm of the whole country. In this backdrop, it will not be an exaggeration to say that Rashtrakavi Dinkar is akin to a cultural heritage of Bharat. In Hindi literature, there is reference to two Rashtrakavis—Rashtrakavi Maithilisharan Gupt and Rashtrakavi Ramdhari Singh Dinkar. The literary output of Dinkarji spread from pre-Independence days to 1973-74. As such, his literature presents a literary view of Bharatiya Independence Movement to the Post-Independence socio-political scenario, including Chinese aggression. The expansive nature of the contents of his writings, especially poetry, highlight his stature as a writer.

As a poet, Dinkarji is ahead of Maithilisharan Gupt, Subhadra Kumari Chauhan, Makhan Lal Chaturvedi, Sohanlal Dwivedi, Shyam Narayan Pandey and other poets of national-cultural stream. The spark of nationalism that Maithilisharan Gupt ignited through the publication of *'Bharat Bharati'* in 1912, was forwarded by Dinkarji through his poems like *'Hunkar'*, *'Renuka'*, *'Rashmirathi'*, *'Parashuram ki Pratiksha'* and *'Kurukshetra'*. Rashtrakavi Dinkar is, on one side, inspired by the

Bharat, a dream that lifts the earth to the heavan,
arat, a thought that ushers the heaven to the earth.
Bharat, a name of detachment, bright self-rise,
arat is the halo of humanity and paramount victory.

ome scholars consider Dinkarji a poet of only mundane rialism. They reckon only that side of Dinkarji's writings e issues of materialism have been seriously raised. This is sided awareness of his writings. The boldness and clarity which he raised materialistic issues, he showed same our in touching upon spiritual issues. This is the reason oved the spiritual consciousness of Gurudev Rabindranath kur. About Gurudev, Dinkarji wrote, "The footfall of t super human, who is above the mundane human, is in every line of Rabindra's poetry, and that footfall has en resounding in Bharatiya literature since eternity". The iritualism running in Bharatiya literature since eternity is esent in Dinkar's cultural thoughts.

Dinkarji was always concerned about the issue of national nguage. He wrote two books on this topic—*'Rashtrabhasha* nd *Rashtriya Ekata'* and *'Rashtrabhasha Andolan and* *andhiji'*. Dinkarji believed that Hindi was made national anguage because only this is capable of keeping intact both cultural unity and geographical indivisibility of the country.

Dinkarji was as great a prose writer as he was a poet. Therefore, a strong voice of nationalism is interwoven in not only his poetry put also prose. Dinkarji had a profound study of Bharatiya culture. His thoughts regarding culture are recorded in two of his treatises—*'Sanskriti Ke Char Adhyay'* and *'Hamari Sanskritik Ekata'*.

Dinkarji put great emphasis on elemental unity of Bharatiya culture. Dinkarji considers spiritiualism as the chief feature and core element of Bharatiya culture. He identified the impact of this specific property of Bharatiya culture as a perceptible influence on the cultures of the world. In the

Vedanta philosophy of Swami Vivekan
side, he is inspired and influenced by
Maharashi Aurobindo and Gurudev R
addition to this, the notion of incessan
tinges the mind and thought of Dinkarji

In his acclaimed anthology of poe
exhorts the youth to offer oblation in
Independendence. He writes.

रण की घड़ी जलन की वेला, तो मैं भी कु
सुलग रही यदि शिखा यज्ञ की, अपना हवन
नए प्रात के अरुण! तिमिर-उर में मरीचि संध
युग के मूक शैल जागो हुंकारों, कुछ गान व

Time of strife bring flashes of burn, I feel li
If crust of holy fire rises, I'll offer my ob
O crimson gleam of new morn! target the core
O mute stones of this Age, arise, bellow and s

Rashtrakavi Dinkar is not satisfied even after
body, heart and life to the nation. Dinkarji is such a
who, for his whole life, created awareness about
and never let his commitment to the nation loosen.
important positions during the government head
Jawaharlal Nehru but when questions were raise
Nehru's wrong policy on Chinese war, Rashtrakav
loudly protested thorugh *'Parashuram Ki Pratiksha'*.

Reading Dinkarji's poetry gives one a feel that el
Bharat to the apex level of accomplishment has ever b
goal. Wishing to see Bharat as mentor of the world, Di
through his poem entitled *'Himalaya'*, gives the messag
only Bharat can herald peace in the world:

भारत एक स्वप्न, भू को ऊपर ले जाने वाला,
भारत एक विचार, स्वर्ग को भू पर ले जाने वाला।
भाख है संज्ञा विराग की, उज्ज्वल आत्म-उदय की,
भारत है आभा मनुष्य की, सबसे बड़े विजय की।

chapter entitted '*Prachin Bharat ke Bauddhik Utkarsh*' in the book entitled '*Hamari Sanskritik Ekata*', Dinkarji has asserted that from BC 480 to AD 700, Bharat's honour was at its peak in the areas of philosophy, mathematics, astrology, medicine etc. In modern times too, Bharatiya literature and philosophy influenced the German people. The transcendental movement of America was influenced by Bharatiya thought. In this way, Dinkarji not only defined the cultural unity of Bharat but also aroused the nascent self-confidence of its people.

In the book entitled '*Sanskriti, Bhasha aur Rashtra*', Dinkarji has contemplated on the mutual relation between language, culture and nation. In this book, he said that cultural races become extinct when they begin to follow other cultures, ignoring their own. He further said that when a human race adopts alien language abandoning its own, it implies shameful cultural slavery. Its natural consequence is that the concerned race loses its distinct personality and its self-respect gradually dies out. In due course, his feeling of patriotism also starts waning.

Thus, it can be safely asserted that Dinkarji was not only a Rashtrakavi but also a herald of Bharatiya culture by virtue of his musings on Bharatiya culture. To conclude, the opinion of Dr. Harivansh Rai Bachchan is worth consideration—"Dinkarji led a rigorous life. His pursuit of literature was unparalleled. Some time back, a gentleman of Kolkata wrote to me as to how appropriate it was to confer Gyanpith Award on him? In my reply I wrote—he would have been duly honoured if he were awarded four Gyanpith separately for prose, poetry, lectures and promotion of Hindi language".

—29 July, 2018

□

Technical Education in Bharat

The prosperity of a country depends on harnessing its natural and human resources for productive industrialisation. For proper utilisation of human resources in trade and industry, science education and development of technical skill are required. *(Scientific Policy Resolution,* 1958; Govt. of Bharat).

There has been a strong tradition of science and technology in Bharatiya civilisation, one of the oldest among world civilisations. Ancient Bharat has been a virtual laboratory of saints, sages, scholars and scientists. Numerous researches have proved that Bharat has been a pioneer in the field of applied science and technology as well as new discoveries in various areas. Prominent contributions of ancient Bharat in this context are the following ones:

- The concept of Zero
- Decimal System
- Numerical Notations
- Theory of Sun-centric Cosmos
- Special Smelting System of Iron and Zinc.

In the wake of foreign aggression and subjugation to the aliens, this knowledge became evanescent, and addition of new knowledge stopped. Since the tradition of such knowledge was abruptly disrupted, the very veracity of its existence in the past is questioned, but the fact remains that their proof in shape of remnants are being discovered and recovered every now and then.

Technical Education in Modern Times

During pre-Independence, technical learning was utilised by the British administrators in construction of building, canal, road, ports etc. in the beginning. The first technical institution opened in 1794 was College of Engineering, Guindy, Chennai. In 1854, a school was opened in Pune for training of engineers. In the then Uttar Pradesh, Thomson Engineering College was opened in Roorkee in 1847.

In the wave of Swadeshi Movement, following the Bang-Bhang movement in 1905, a Bharatiya Shiksha Parishad was constituted and through this, it was demanded that technical university inspired by indigenous treasure of knowledge should be opened. The Bharatiya Education Council opened College of Engineering and Technology at Jadavpur in 1908. Similary, in 1917, Pt. Madan Mohan Malaviya became instrumental in starting the departments of Mechanical, Electrical and Metallurgical engineering in Banaras Hindu University.

Viewing the significance of technical education for economic and material development of the country, All India Council of Technical Education (AICTE) was formed in 1945. In 1956, engineering colleges, one each in Kolkata, Mumbai and Chennai, were opened. Under National Education Policy-1986, AICTE was entrusted the responsibility of planning, policy making, creation of standard, qualitative education, creation of funds for the primary area, evaluation and monitoring, certification, institution of awards etc. to ensure co-ordinated development of technical education in the country.

Post globalisation, Bharat has witnessed rapid expansion of technical eduction. A glance at the data of higher education reveals that after Arts stream, technical education is at the next position. The figures for 2019 show that there were 10426 technical institutions in which more than 35 lakh students studied. The picture in figures looks impressive, but the quality of end products is disappointing. When we examine the products on the standards of quality and employability, we confront the awful truth.

The Scenario of Technical Education in Bharat
Engineering Education

Graduate/ UG	Number of Institutions			Sanctioned Admission			Actual Admission		
	2015-16	2016-17	2017-18	15-16	16-17	17-18	2015-16	16-17	17-18
	3365	3285	3225	1630850	1554050	1476428	835073	785554	750206
Post Graduate/ UG	**Number of Institutions**			**Sanctioned Admission**			**Actual Admission**		
	2015-16	2016-17	2017-18	15-16	16-17	17-18	2015-16	16-17	17-18
	2304	2231	2138	207325	196976	186042	87109	69282	68560
Diploma	**Number of Institutions**			**Sanctioned Admission**			**Actual Admission**		
	2015-16	2016-17	2017-18	15-16	16-17	17-18	2015-16	16-17	17-18
	3850	3926	3918	1255569	1244958	1208518	713044	705037	667664
Total	**9518**	**9442**	**9281**	**3093744**	**2995983**	**2870988**	**1635226**	**1559873**	**1486430**

Technical Education Comprises Architecture, Town Planning, Management, Hotel Management, Pharmacy etc.

Source: AICPE

From a glance at the figure quoted above, it comes out that in technical education, which is at the second position in the country, the numbers of technical institutions and total enrolment are steadily diminishing after 2015. Actual admission in these institutions were limited to 60 per cent of the sanctioned strength. In some institutions, the figure of admission is zero.

An investigative survey on 'Employability of Engineers' accomplished by an organisation named Inspiring Minds reveals that in the Information Technology Sector—on which we feel pride and which is the main area of our investment and income—the ability status of qualified engineers is such that only 4.77 per cent of them are capable of writing correct logic of any computer programme. Around 60 per cent of students under survey wrote such codes which could not be applied to system. Only 1.4 per cent students could write workable programmes. The availability of employment in traditional branches of engineering like chemical, mechanical, and electronics is respectively 1.64, 5.5, 6.48 and 7.7 per cent. According to a report of Mackenzie, submitted a decade ago, only 25 per cent of engineers of Bharat deserved employment.

According to Shri C.P. Gurunani, the CEO of Tech Mahindra, the leading IT company of Bharat, "As per NASSCOM, we will need 6 million (60 lakh) personnel trained in cyber security, but there is a great dearth of such skilled specialists, which has become a big challenge for us. The onus of skill development and market development is now being shifted to the industry. It is evident from this that the education students are receiving from their colleges or universities is not useful for industry. In this backdrop, big companies are setting up their own training centres, where their engineers are made worthy of employment."

Employability Percentage of Engineering Graduates in Different Roles.

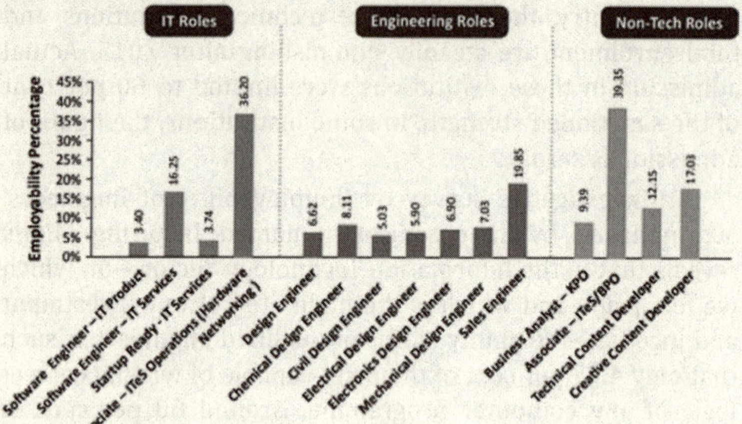

In the above graph, it has been indicated the varied areas or sectors in which the bachelors of technology are gainfully employed. The data reveal that people with bachelor's degree in technology are engaged more in non-technical fields.

This scenario of technical education raises a pertinent question as to what are the basic problems and drawbacks of technical education that produce engineers with low employability? The issue points out many valid reasons. Of these, the important ones are, poor teacher-student ratio, low academic standard of teachers, and lack of quality standard of entrance tests. After selection of teachers through academic tests and interview, there is no system in place for their in-service training, orientation and refresher programmes. As its natural result, the research work done by them is not upto the mark.

In engineering colleges, the teacher-student ratio should be between 1:12 and 1:15, but in our country it is 1:25. This tells upon the quality of teaching in classroom. Shortage of faculty in position is another important problem. In IITs of the country, taken together, there is a shortage of 34% teachers.

In the IITs of Goa, Dharwad, Kharagpur, Kanpur and Delhi, there is shortage of 62, 47, 46, 37 and 29 per cent respectively (*source*: Ministry of Human Resource, Govt. of Bharat, 31st March, 2018). As an immediate measure, the vacant post of teachers should be filled, besides preparing syllabus and courses for teacher education in technical faculty.

Teacher-Student Ratio

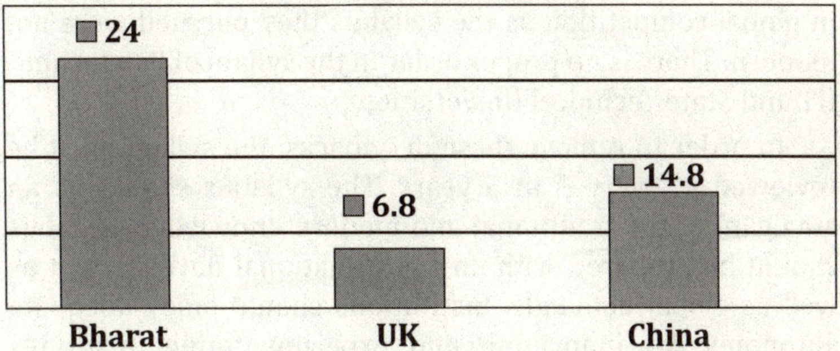

A system needs to be visualised and created to inspire and lure the students of premier engineering colleges to adopt teaching profession.

Basic infrastructure of the engineering colleges is also an important issue to address. Lack of state-of-the-art laboratories, latest machinery and equipments for practical classes, rich library, facility of e-learning etc. affect the right atmosphere for academic pursuit. Other problcms are lack of collaboration with industry and regular review of syllabus which are making the courses of most of the colleges irrelevant in the changed times.

It is necessary that for development of basic infrastructure a pragmatic project, with timeline for implementation, should be prepared forthwith in consultation, co-ordination and dialogue with industry. Some interface between industry and institution is visible in National Institutes of Technology of Bharat. The Government of Bharat had constituted U.R. Rao Committee in 2003 to consider ways and means to ensure industry-institution interface so that seats in the branches of engineering may be fixed in proportion to requirements. The report of committee is still pending with the government.

The cardinal problem of technical education of Bharat is that the curriculum is not comprehensive. There is no uniformity in the syllabus followed by different universities. There does not exist an effective system to review the syllabus periodically. Engineering graduates are falling behind others in global competition as the syllabus they pursued were not modern. There is no proper order in the syllabi of Polytechnic, IIT and State Technical Universities.

In order to remove these drawbacks, the syllabi must be reviewed at every 3 to 5 years. The syllabus should be an amalgam of the traditional and modern knowledge. Syllabus should be prepared with an eye to national development as well as global demands. Institutions should enjoy adequate autonomy for innovation and experimentation. Institutes should provide platform for interaction among institutions, teachers and students, both separately and together. In such interactions, there should be an exchange of innovations and experimentations done in different institutions.

The model curriculum prepared by AICTE has included Environmental Science, Moral Values, Bharatiya Constitution, Bharatiya Traditional Knowledge and Training as non-credit courses, whereas these deserve the status of credit courses. The entrance test for engineering colleges should include Hindi and other Bharatiya languages,. Basic books, materials for e-learning, test contents and libraries should be available in Bharatiya languages. In our view, in all genres of technical education, there should be an option of Bharatiya languages for teaching and learning. Social sensitisation of engineering students should be done through programme like 'Unnat Bharat Abhiyan'. Colleges should be linked to adjacent villages, which the institutions should adopt for social and educational upliftment of the populace.

Technical Research At Global Level

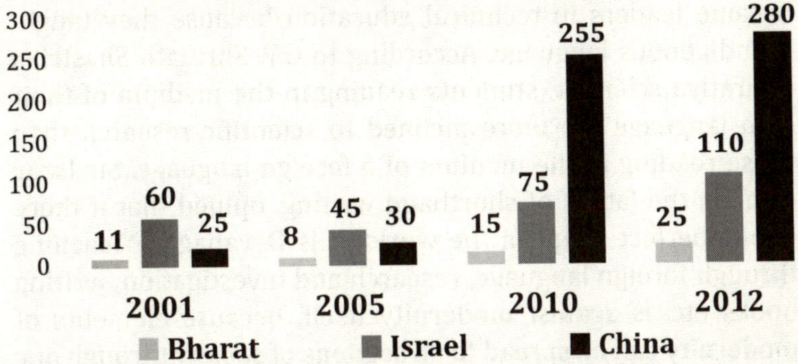

The bulk of research work in the field of engineering is very small in comparison to that in China and Israel. The reason of Bharat lagging behind other countries lies in lack of quality education, inadequate physical infrastructure, English being the only language of technical research-writing and weak motivation for research work. Hence it is necessary to promote research and investigation for better academic output.

A new problem is surfacing of late—on the one side, the government is opening new IITs, NITs IIITs, and on the other side, student enrolment is falling sharply. The students taking JEE Advanced examination after qualifying JEE Mains are small in number. The data for the years 2016, 2017 and 2018 show that respectively 31, 23 and 32 per cent candidates who qualified in JEE Mains, abstained from JEE Advanced examination. Students prefer prominent engineering college to the new IITs. The main reason behind this is poor academic quality and physical infrastructure in new institutions of national level.

This discussion will remain incomplete without mentioning the fact that engineering courses are not conducted in the medium of indigenous languages. This is so in face of the fact that comprehension of subject leading to knowledge can never be as effectively possible in an alien language as it is in one's own language. Israel, Germany, Japan, Korea etc. became leaders in technical education because they taught in indigenous language. According to C.V. Shrinath Shastri, a Bharatiya scientist, students reading in the medium of their own language are more inclined to scientific research than those reading in the medium of a foreign language. Sir Isaac Pitman, the father of shorthand writing, opined that if there is one perfect script in the world, it is Devanagari. Teaching through foreign language, research and investigation, writing books etc. is against modernity itself, because elements of modernity can be spread to all sections of society through our own language.

A review of the entire educational system of the country reveals that our technical education is qualitatively weak, and for the last four or five years, it is registering steep quantitative fall also. It is imperative for the government and society to earnestly think about quality enhancement of technical education and to initiate concrete measures in this regard.

References:

1. Science, Medicine, Technology in Ancient India
2. All India Council of Technical Education
3. Human Resource Development Ministry
4. IIT Kharagpur in Connecting the Dots Between Ancient India and Modern Science.

—3 March, 2019

□

Curriculum and Nature of Management Education

If we have to review the present state of the curriculum of management as a subject, we will have to consider the bitter truth that not even 25 per cent of the graduates and postgraduates passing out from management institutes of the country are worthy of any employment. Similar reports of some studies and surveys have been published. The root cause of this sad state is the nature of curriculum of management education as of now, compounded by the utterly aimless education system of the country. As such, students and distinguished scholars feel an urgency to initiate the process to review the current curriculum of management and to adapt it to the specific needs of our country.

The Delor's committee of UNESCO has said in its report that, "The pattern or structure of any country's education should be compatible to the country's culture and development." We have added one word to it and pronounced that, "Education of the country should be accordant to its culture, nature and development." At the same time, we feel that while framing a curriculum it is pertinent to consider the base of the past, the needs of the present, and the possibilities of the future. The curriculum of management needs to be considered in the light of these facts.

Management is an integration of material or worldly as well as economic resources with human potential to meet specific needs. Man is the nucleus of the integration of these three components, because such an integration is, after all, effected by man only. The perspective of the integration of human potential should be spiritual. As such, a proper, meaningful and successful management is possible only through a balanced integration of the material and the spiritual components.

In the contemporary modern world, the manager has an important role. A modern manager is under enormous pressure of work, he follows a tight time schedule, he is required to fulfil numerous expectations. He works in an atmosphere of cut-throat competition. Living far from his family, he is under deep mental stress. He faces the challenge to adapt himself to the demands of such changing situations and to accommodate new dimensions of management, so that, even in the stressful situations he may, while maintaining his health and cool of mind, perform his duties efficiently and, at the same time, contribute to the welfare of the humanity, society and nation. In this backdrop, we need to produce brilliant managers who infuse in their profession high morality and values of life. The new curriculum must take into consideration these requirements. Therefore, the following points merit serious consideration.

Self-Management and Holistic Development

If we have to effectively manage anything from family to the country, or from small shops to big business and industry, the key-person will be an efficient manager. In the current curriculum of management this basic ingredient seems missing. This needs to be compensated by a holistic development of budding managers undergoing the course. For this, the concept of *Panch Kosh* propounded in the *Taittiriya Upanishad* will have to be made the base, which will ensure life-force vitality, besides physical, intellectual and spiritual development. (Ref: *Uchch Shiksha : Bharatiya Drishti*; *Atmatatva Ka Vistar*).

Apart from this, self-management should include stress management, health management, environmental management, financial management, family management and time management.

Stress Management

Now-a-days even a common man is leading a stressful life. In such a situation, the manager of the organisation has himself to stay free from stress and keep his co-workers also completely stress-free. For this, the curriculum needs to include yoga. At work place the business firms must provide for a yoga enclave for employees. The *Shrimadbhagvat Gita* says–*Yoga Karmashu Kaushalam*–which means that complete focus on, and dedication to action, leads to successful execution of task. The basis of concentration is yoga.

Financial Management

Man power and financial resources are the foundation of any organisation. Hence it is necessary that the manager has adequate expertise in financial management.

Environmental Management

Industry has a considerable share in creating environmental menace in the country and the world. In order to generate awareness about environment in personal, familial and occupational life, environmental management should be a part of the curriculum of management. Different aspects and dimensions of management should specially emphasise environment conservation.

Health Management

Now-a-days, health-problems are increasing day by day, mainly because of bad food habits environmental pollution and stressful life. To ensure that the manager is himself hale and hearty, proper health management becomes a highly relevant issue.

Family Management

The concept of family is the greatest distinguishing feature of Bharat. This concept embodies within it definitive solution of a majority of problems facing the individual and his class. Right from the individual's family to his industry, business, organisation etc should have a strong feeling of belonging to a family. The managing director to common personnel and workers in a business or industry should be bound by the feeling of being a family. The possibility of conflict is minimum in an organisation where all are knit together, and virtue of co-ordination leads to natural solution of issues.

Time Management

In order to carry out all types of management enumerated above, time management is compulsory. God has given equal respect to all – the poor, the rich, the worker, the owner etc – hence, keeping this element in management, more work can be accomplished in less time, and work can be finished on schedule, which keeps the manager free from stress. It is, therefore, necessary to include time management in the curriculum so that managers are capable of discharging their onerous duties efficiently

Personal Working Style and Organisational Behaviour

Management is a psychological issue, therefore manager needs to be a psychologist too. Hence, psychology as a subject must be a component of the curriculum of management. The important elements in the manager's personal working style are—collectiveness, anonymity, co-operation and transparency, which are enumerated below:

Collectiveness: Collectiveness implies the quality of moving or working together. For this, equitable treatment of one and all is necessary. There was a time when a dictum was very popular—'Boss is always right'. But nowadays, teamwork is more acceptable from all view points. No individual can ever be perfect. All of us are individually imperfect, but collectively we can become perfect

Likewise, the more the decision-making is collective, the more will it be flawless. As such, the efficiency of the management lies in ensuring direct and indirect participation of more and more people in decision-making.

Anonymity: Giving credit to co-workers for success is a noble managerial practice. It is justified because success in every task is always a result of participation of many people in it. At the same time one should keep the positive mindset of owning the responsibility for failure. It is required to build an atmosphere of, 'we, ours, us and ourselves' in place of 'I, my mine and myself'.

Co-operation and Togetherness: It is necessary to develop an attitude of co-operation and collaboration. The manager should have a tendency to make effective groups of small number of people. Wherever there is something weak or missing, the manager's role is to fill the gap. Every, individual has some qualities, but at the same time some weaknesses too. Manager should harness the qualities of his colleagues for productive work of the organisation and compensate for weaknesses in them.

Transparency: There should be transparency in every work of the organisation. About financial transaction it is wisely said—'Account should be right, and it should look right too.' There should be honesty, sanctity and credibility in business and industry, and this should be visible also. The manager should exemplify this from his personal conduct.

Inclusion of Traditional Bharatiya Knowledge:

Question may arise as to the efficacy of Bharatiya knowledge tradition. Is it needed simply because this is our traditional knowledge? This is not a logical assertion. Bharatiya knowledge is required because in the West people start groping for solution when a crisis arises, but in Bharat our thinkers have been proactive to the extent that they thought over the issues which were to appear in distant future, and suggested their solution. Yoga was prescribed to prevent people from stress and environmental conservation was recommended much before global warming appeared. Our Bharatiya Literature includes literature many such strands of knowledge and wisdom. Hence, Bharatiya knowledge tradition is efficacious not only for Bharat but for the entire world.

In the traditional Bharatiya knowledge we come across

many examples of successful management in the treatises like the *SriMadbhagvat Gita* and the *Ramayana* In the life of icons like Shivaji, Chanakya etc we see effective management skill that naturally impress us. In the *Ramayana*, Shri Ram, despite being deficient in resources, vanquished *Ravan* who was capable in all aspects. When we analyse its reasons, we find in him golden features of self-management and human resource management like, quality of taking all along, no discrimination between the high and the low, affectionate behaviour with all, standing firm on truth in adverse circumstances, working patiently without getting dejected even in adverse situation etc. we should include in the curriculum of Management, all such important and useful examples available in our ancient treatises.

Many scholars have written books devoted to Management in the *Gita*, Management in the *Ramayana,* Management of Chanakya etc. But such ideas have never been included in the curriculum in the perspectives of modern needs. In Japan, elements of effective management found in *Shri Madbhagvat Gita* have been incorporated in the curriculum of Management.

Modern Dimensions of Management

Nowadays, various Experiments are being done in many countries of the world in the specific field of management to fit it in the contemporary requirement. For example, Japan has identified seven aspects or tiers of management for its study— (i) Strategy (ii) Structure (iii) System (iv) Staff (v) Style (vi) Skills (vii) Sublime Goal—all bound intrinsically by the notion of 'Come Together—Think Together—Work Together.'

After studying the curriculum of other countries, we can choose useful material from them suitable for our country. Viewed in the context of our country, relevant aspects of management that strike to us are— (i) Waste Management (plastic garbage and hardware garbage) (ii) Water Management (iii) Sustainable Development Management (iv) Agriculture Management (v) Transport Management (vi)

Disaster Management (vii) Health Management (viii) Family Management (ix) Human Resource Management etc. Likewise, various dimensions of management in view of societal and regional needs may also be added.

In present times there are two global problems– development and employment. There is little co-ordination amongst development and employment. Physical and material development is globally increasing, but unemployment and poverty are also proportionately increasing. This is a big challenge for the scholars of development economics. If steps are taken to remove unemployment and poverty, development is affected. If development is accelerated, unemployment and poverty grow. In the same way there is a similar difficulty in maintaining equilibrium in development and environment. A country like America is also ignoring environmental conservation for sake of physical and material development. In the past, Bharat has been successful in maintaining a balance between such baffling issues. In the present too, Bharat can follow a similar management system to set an example and give a direction to the whole world.

Case Studies

In the present curriculum of management, only non-Bharatiya case studies are being taught as illustration. The illustrations which are not related to social or economic realities of Bharat fail to inspire students and also to drive home the relevant message. As a result these become difficult for students to comprehend and retain in memory. A negative conclusion impression that comes out from such case studies is that impressive examples of effective management are not available in our country, or no such examples were there in the past too. Without efficient management how could such a big country's vast and various machinery be properly run? It is an irony that when foreigners visited Bharat to study Tiffin Service Management of Mumbai and impeccable Logistic Management of the Kumbh Fair, the Indian Institute(s) of Management, for the first time, became aware of their academic importance. As such, it is imperative to include native case studies in the curriculum. Hence, it is imperative that exemplary native experiments should be included in the curriculum for case studies. However, suitable examples from foreign countries may also be included.

Spirituality and Inclusion of Values: According to Swami Vivekananda, doing any work with selfless detachment amounts to spirituality. Simultaneously, recognising only real self by realising ones taste, nature, weakness and speciality leads to spirituality. Students should introspect and ponder over the issue like who am I, what is the justification of my existence, what is the aim of my life etc. Such an introspection will sharpen their social compassion and encourage them to undertake social service. How these should be included in the curriculum, merits our serious consideration.

From this angle Japan's Principle of Kaizen is important :

Man is not a problem. He is beset with problems. Solve them.

Problem cannot be solved by blaming or criticising someone.

People have to find out the solution to problems.

One should execute one's responsibility. One should begin one's work by oneself.

Regular self-appraisal is required.

Scholars who have a Bharatiya vision and who have read ancient Bharatiya treatises have also expressed such opinion. Prof Subir Choudhary, ex-Director, Management Institute, Kolkata says,

" We will have to move towards our base once again".

In order to move forward in the direction enumerated above, it is necessary to adopt values. Maharshi Aurobindo opined" , **"Since the time country's education was divorced from life-values, the country's populace lost its direction**

and righteousness." In Bharatiya tradition religion, economy, sensuality and salvation find a balanced vision. We consider economy and sensuality as important components of worldly life, but salvation can be attained only if economy and sensuality are rooted in righteousness.

Do we need separate books for value education? No, not at all. Value education can be given by including values in the textbooks, by conducting co-curricular activities, through ideal ambience of the campus and inspiring personal life of teachers

Synthesis of Pragmatism and Experimentation

In the subjects being taught today, there should be inclusion of both theoretical and practical knowledge. It has become imperative to seriously think on changing the style and method of teaching by adding due emphasis on subject based activities and hands-on experience through field visits. In this context it is necessary to think about novel project work related to students' subjects under study. Students pursuing a course in Water Management may be made to undertake project in villages facing water crisis. Most of our students become unsuccessful in professional life for want of practical knowledge.

Bharatiya Languages as Medium of Instruction

Language is another important dimension of teaching-learning, which may appear difficult to tackle. Presently, the medium of teaching of Management course is only English. It is imperative, therefore, that the syllabus of Management and its study material should, in the first place, be prepared in Hindi, and gradually in other Bharatiya languages. We are aware of the fact that all the countries which are economically developed, are imparting education in their own languages. Some time back the University Grants Commission issued an advisory to all universities to conduct Management courses in the medium of Hindi. At the same time, teaching of Management should be started in other Bharatiya languages also. The National Education Policy too emphasises dual language mode in all courses of higher education. Unless and until teaching is done in students' own language, they may score marks by cramming the answer but they cannot gain real knowledge.

The Art of Teaching

In the Bharatiya Tradition there were thirty-two modes or methods of reading. Of these, only one is popularly in use today, which is lecture mode. When we consider it from the angle of students' mental development, we feel that with students' mobility to higher grades of formal education, the lecture mode should proportionate decrease in use. The addition of inputs like dialogue, debate, question and answer, practical work, co-curricular and extra-curricular activities etc. need to be included in management education. In the same way, hands-on experience like surveys, regional studies, rural visits etc. should also be used as academic tools of teaching and learning.

In this brief write-up I have identified only some changes required in management courses. I shall be the last person to believe that what I have proposed is the best, and therefore, final and conclusive. What is required is that management gurus and managers in business and industry should deliberate on the issue, leading to the framing of a curriculum of management which is capable of addressing the needs and aspiration of society and the country, while ushering the whole world into a new era of management education.

—12 July, 2017

□□□